Introdu

How did a youngster from the Eastern lowlands of Kenya, who was too shy to speak in his school's Christian Union, grow up to become one of Africa's foremost evangelists?

In this warm and moving account of his life, Stephen Mbogo reveals how an evangelist is 'made', beginning with his own rapturous response to Jesus Christ, and how he nurtured and grew that relationship until the sheer joy of it was too much to keep to himself.

Converted as a teenager at high school, and passionate about missions throughout university, Stephen knew early-on that God was calling him to be an evangelist and preacher. Unfortunately, his parents were horrified. They wanted him to get a 'real man's job'!

Yet the 'calling' persisted. Slowly God's call came into clearer focus: Stephen was to spend his life mobilising the churches, or 'the reached' of Africa, in order for them together to take the gospel to 'the unreached'. He was to use 'the possible' of the few resources they might have, to attempt 'the impossible', for God would then provide.

This is the fascinating true story of how that 'calling' came true.

Stephen has led missions to tens of thousands across the continent of Africa. He played a behind-the-scene role in launching the National Prayer Breakfasts for both Kenya and South Sudan. Recently, he has also participated as one of the speakers in the European Union Prayer Breakfast.

Today Stephen heads up African Enterprise, a missions agency working through ten teams across Africa – evangelising the cities of Africa in word and deed.

He is also:
Chairman, Lausanne (EPSA) English, Portuguese and Spanish speaking Africa;
Chairman Movement Day Africa;
Chairman Proclaim 2020: Congress of African Evangelists from all 54 Nations;
and
Chairman Mission Africa: Follow-up on Lausanne Cape Town 2010 (Africa's) commitments.

Also by Stephen Mbogo:

Values and Motivations for Leadership: A focus on the Legislators of the first South Sudan Legislative Assembly

Also by Anne Coomes:

Festo Kivengere – a biography
Out of the Black Shadows (with Stephen Lungu)
African Harvest – the story of African Enterprise

Send Me To The Nations

*'From the reached to the unreached
From the possible to the impossible'*

Stephen Mbogo
with Anne Coomes

african harvest
PUBLICATIONS

First published in Great Britain in 2020

African Harvest Publications
PO Box 236
Macclesfield SK10 4GJ

Copyright © Stephen Mbogo 2020

The right of Stephen Mbogo and Anne Coomes to be identified as the authors of this work has been asserted by them in accordance with the Copyright, Designs and Patents Act 1988. All rights reserved.

Cover and logo design by Deborah Noble 2020.
The right of Deborah Noble to be identified as artist of this work has been asserted by her in accordance with the Copyright, Designs and Patents Act 1988. All rights reserved.

Cover portrait in pastels of Stephen Mbogo and pen-and-watercolour illustrations by William Mather, 2020 www.williammatherart.com
The right of William Mather to be identified as artist of this work has been asserted by him in accordance with the Copyright, Designs and Patents Act 1988. All rights reserved.

All rights reserved. No part of this book may be reproduced or transmitted in any form or by any means, electronic or mechanical, including photocopying, recording, or by any information storage and retrieval system without permission in writing from the publisher.

Quotations taken from The Holy Bible, New International Version (Anglicized edition).
Copyright © 1979, 1984, 2011 by Biblica.
Used by permission of Hodder & Stoughton Ltd, a Hachette UK Company. All rights reserved.
'NIV' is a registered trademark of Biblica. UK trademark number 1448790.

British Library Cataloguing-in-Publication Data
A catalogue record for this book is available from the British Library.

African Harvest Publications is a publishing imprint of
Parish Pump Publishing, PO Box 236 Macclesfield SK10 4GJ

ISBN 978-0-9932130-1-4

Typesetting and Book Layout by Arnold Kedenge, Light the World Intl. Ltd. Nairobi
arnoldkedenge@gmail.com   +254 702 102 490

Printing by Publish4All Nairobi
P4akenya@gmail.com   +254 798 674 454

Distributed by African Harvest Publications
office@africanharvestpublications.co.uk

Dedication

For my Dad and Mum - Eustace and Priscilla Mbogo. Your love and support made everything possible for me.

Contents

Introduction	i
Dedication	v
Foreword	1
1 My Mother's Love	5
2 Finding Jesus at Kangaru	21
3 What happens now?	41
4 Daystar University	53
5 'Who do you love most?'	71
6 Mission to Moyale – Called to The Frontiers	81
7 African Enterprise	97
8 The Girl in the Red Jacket	111
9 AE Missions Director, Kenya	125
10 Learning to Trust God for Everything	141
11 Further Studies and Parenthood	161
12 Our Ordination, First Church and School	171
13 Team Leader for Kenya	187
14 National Prayer Breakfast for South Sudan	199
15 Doing our Doctorates at Biola University	215
Epilogue	249

Foreword

When God called me to launch African Enterprise back in the early 60s, Africa was in a maelstrom of change. Across the continent, countries were gaining their independence. There was endless energy and burgeoning populations, but little moral compass. Widespread corruption, selfish leadership and many vested power interests were poisoning the new countries. Millions of lives were being broken. Africa needed Jesus Christ.

Nowhere was this situation more critical than in the cities of Africa, and among the leadership of Africa. For they were the powerhouses that would both drive and steer Africa into her future. Reach them for Christ, and the continent could be transformed.

In July 1961 I walked on the beach in Liberia. I was 24 and had a crazy dream that had become the passion of my life: to take the news of Jesus Christ to every city in Africa. In all of Africa. AE was just a little fledgling in the nest then, but we were aiming to fly very high: to fulfill the evangelisation of Africa through word and deed in partnership with the Church. That morning on the beach I drew a big outline of Africa on the sand, and I asked God to give me 50 years of ministry, one for every state that was then in Africa. He answered my prayer in abundance.

50 years later, my time was up! African Enterprise was going strong, but at 76, I was wearing out. In 2004 my beloved brother, Stephen Lungu, had taken over from me as International Team Leader, and had done an incredible job for eight years. It was now approaching 2012, and both Stephen Lungu and I felt it was time to hand on the baton to a younger leader, who had the same God-given passion for the leadership and cities of Africa.

God answered our prayers. He gave us the Revd Dr Stephen Mbogo, who has fulfilled the job spec beyond our dreams. He is truly the man to lead African Enterprise in Africa today, where the problems now threatening the Continent are just so great. I regularly thank God for Stephen in my prayers.

AE had first met Stephen in the early 1990s, when he was a young graduate straight out of Daystar University in Nairobi. He had been strongly recommended to us by the Fellowship of Christian Unions, who sent him over to meet Gershon Mwiti, our Kenyan Team Leader. Stephen told Gershon that he wanted to preach and evangelise, and so Gershon dumped him in at the deep end on a mission, to see how he would do. Gershon liked what he saw of Stephen very much, and Stephen joined our Kenyan staff that autumn.

I first worked with Stephen in 1994, on a big mission to Harare. Stephen had nearly been killed a short time before by some robbers in Nairobi, and the story of his miraculous escape, and his ability to share his faith with the crowds in Harare made a deep impression on me. I could see a young man whose faith in God was profound.

In the months and years that followed, I heard great things about Stephen from various senior AE staff. They spoke of his gift for evangelism, his organisational skills, his willingness to work hard, his attention to detail, and his ability to get on with people from all walks of life, from the Vice-President of Kenya (!) to the children in the slums, where he and his wife pastored a church at the weekends. He became our Team Leader for Kenya and was a great success. He was the only team leader we had ever had who played a significant role in setting up two National Prayer Breakfasts, for Kenya and South Sudan. Not a bad record for someone still in his 30s!

But then, in 2008, Stephen left us to go to America, to do his doctorate. We wished him every success, but in AE he was very much missed.

Roll the film forward four years, and in 2012 it dawned on us that

Foreword

Stephen's doctorate at Biola should be nearly completed by now, and he might be thinking of coming home. The more we thought about this, the more excited we got. We knew Stephen's commitment to Jesus Christ, but we also knew he had an inclusive style of leadership, a willingness to listen and connect with others, total integrity, endless patience, true humility, steady nerves, and a good sense of humour!

We approached him with bated breath: with his doctorate, he could choose a bright future anywhere. Would he even consider moving back to us, and taking on a job of enormous responsibility, endless demands, and never-ending challenges? Having the oversight of ten teams of evangelists working with hundreds of churches in cities across Africa, and also targeting the leadership of those cities for Christ, is not a job for the faint-hearted!

Stephen and Rosemary said YES! And on that day in 2012, African Enterprise celebrated the best news we had had for years. We had found our new CEO.

It was a sheer joy to commission Stephen and Rosemary at the 50th anniversary of AE in August of 2012. I knew that with Stephen Mbogo as International CEO, the future of African Enterprise was in excellent hands.

Why has God blessed Stephen with such prominence and responsibility? I believe the answer goes back many decades, to Stephen's private life: to his personal commitment to hours of prayer, to soaking up the Bible, and to obeying God. He was growing strong spiritual muscles many years before he ever took to the public stage. He is a tool well prepared for his Master's use.

Michael Cassidy
Founder, African Enterprise
Pietermaritzburg
February 2020

'I was curious about everything but school!'

1
My Mother's Love

*'Now choose life, so that you and your children
may live... love the Lord your God...'
- Deuteronomy 30:19,20.*

"Mrs Mbogo, are you Stephen's mother? Your son Stephen is very foolish. We have tried and tried, but he learns nothing. We can't help him. He will be a failure. You need to know that now."

Except for my mother's little gasp of dismay, the dusty classroom was silent. The pupils of Temple Road Primary School in Nyeri had all gone home for the day. The teacher looked tired and exasperated, and obviously wanted to go home, too. But first, she had summoned my mother and I to come into school after hours. She wanted to talk to her about me. About how I was failing maths and just about every other subject they tried to teach me.

"Your son is simply stupid," the teacher said again. "He will never get beyond primary school. If he even gets that far!"

It was 1974, I was seven years old and the first crisis of my life had arrived. As my mother hurried me home, she was crying; I was feeling shamed but wondering what the fuss was all about.

Our family name, Mbogo, means 'buffalo'. It conveys the idea of something solid and substantial. But as a child, I was more of a butterfly. Our family's recent move from Embu to Nyeri, up into the

Central Highlands of Kenya, and one of the oldest colonial towns in Kenya, had awoken the spirit of adventure in me. I was constantly outside, eager to explore the gardens and countryside beyond, to hunt for birds and play my favourite sport – soccer! I was curious about everything except what happened in school. Lessons and homework were boring in comparison, so I hardly gave them a thought.

During the holidays, I was busy enjoying learning to herd my grandfather's cows and goats. This was really fun. We also had the locally much-loved 'money game' where whoever skilfully hit the coin chosen by the rest collected all the coins for himself!

Despite what the teacher had said about me, I had managed to learn one other lesson both very well and very fast: keep an eye on those goats! For neighbouring farmers would chase you when your goats invaded their gardens, and if they got hold of you they would give you a beating.

At home that night, after the teacher warned my mother, my parents stayed up late. I could hear them talking long after I was sent to bed in disgrace. I felt miserable to know that all this trouble was because of me. What I could not know, as I was simply too young to understand, was just how awful my failure at school was for them.

My father Eustace

To understand that, you have to know my father, Eustace. For our family name, Mbogo, or 'buffalo' is a excellent description of my father. He is strong, substantial and determined. Very determined! Once he has set his mind to something, he never gives up. It is good when a son can be proud of his father, and I have always had good reason to be proud of mine. Eustace needed to be a 'buffalo' in order to overcome some enormous obstacles in his early life, and to get as far as he has done. But his success was never attained by trampling on other people. Instead, he has always encouraged others to also improve their lives. In return, they have loved and respected him.

My father comes from the Mbeere tribe of Embu County, high in the foothills of Mount Kenya. That means that I, also, am of the Mbeere tribe. You will almost certainly never have heard of us: the Mbeere tribe is so small that when Kenya lists its 43 tribes, we Mbeere never even get a mention. No wonder that when I first met Rosemary (my wife) at university, and told her "I am a Mbeere" – she laughed and replied: "what's that?" My tribe had not made it to the university circles!

My father grew up in a remote village called Kanyuambora in what was known as the Weru (wilderness or unclaimed land) of Embu County during the 1950s. It was a time of great change: Kenya had become a British colony in 1920 and was headed for independence, which happened in 1963. The country was developing fast, and unheard-of opportunities were appearing. As a young man, my father could see that getting an education would be critical for his future, and so he and his parents grabbed every opportunity and saved every penny in order to get him through primary school.

When my father was then offered a place at a secondary school in our capital city Nairobi, he sacrificed everything in order to get down to the city. He had no money to rent a room of his own, and so he ventured into the slums and rented the tiny space under his fellow tribe-mate's bunkbed, in an already crowded, tiny shack. He slept on the ground under that bunkbed for many months. It was awful when the man just inches above him was drunk! To this day he makes us laugh by sharing his experiences when the 'man above' at times peed in his drunken stupor!

But my father accepted the hardship because he had a great purpose that kept him going: he wanted his high school certificate to enable him to pursue his ultimate goal – a degree. But, upon passing his secondary school he still needed a further two years of high school before college. As the chances for this were at that time limited in Nairobi, he chose to cross the border into our neighbouring nation,

Uganda. In its capital, Kampala, there were more schools.

Unfortunately, my father lacked even the fare for the train, so on the way to Kampala, when the train conductor came down through the carriages, he hid himself in the toilet. When he finally arrived in Kampala, my father discovered he could not even afford a place in the slums. So he went a little way outside of the city, and hired himself out as a part-time farm-hand in exchange for a little money and somewhere to sleep, as he pursued his studies.

A couple of years later, with his high school completed, my father returned to Kenya, and carried on with his education. His first diploma was from the Kenya Institute of Administration (KIA). It was famous throughout Kenya in the early 1960s for its success in preparing young people for the Kenyan Civil Service. The KIA helped my father in another big way, for it was here that he met my mother.

In later years my father would go on to the UK to study at both Reading and Edinburgh Universities, where he was awarded his Master's Degree. He was among the very first ever from our Mbeere tribe to hold a Master's degree, and was thus greatly respected among our people. Many of them looked up to him as being a great encouragement and inspiration for others to pursue their education.

Meanwhile, with his diploma from KIA, my father landed his first job as a respectable government administrator in the Department of Social Affairs in Embu. Embu is about 120 kilometres northeast of Nairobi, and as the main commercial centre for the area, it was a good place to begin a first proper job and have a first proper home. He married my mother, and they moved to Embu to begin their life together.

My mother Priscilla

My mother, Priscilla, comes from the Kamba tribe, in Machakos County. Her father was a soldier with the Kenyan Army, and was very respected locally as he had actually fought for the British Army in both Egypt and Burma during the Second World War. Priscilla was more fortunate than my father had been, for education came easier for her: her father was able to pay for her to go to school, and then on to KIA, where she had met my father.

After graduation and marriage, my mother had got a good job as the catering manager in Embu's community development centre. At that time the local government was keen to help people learn more about farming and general self-care, and so they would invite them to come in from the farms and villages round about, and offer them training in better hygiene, farming skills, cooking skills, and how to take better care of their babies.

Life was good in Embu in the late 1960s and early seventies: both my father and my mother loved working with people, and both had a very positive outlook on life. Young and determined, they took it for granted that they would work hard to make the most of their lives. They looked forward to beginning their family.

I was the first to arrive, on 20th November 1967 and was named Njeru. In due course three sisters would follow me – Lillian, Rachel and Elizabeth, and then another son, Joseph. Our family life was stable, calm and affectionate. We children knew we were loved by our parents and had a dad who was a disciplinarian. We felt secure.

In the following months after the teacher warned my mother, I was to learn just HOW much my parents loved me. They could not bear the thought of me failing at school. They knew all too well what a dismal life I would have without an education.

So, my mother grew determined to help me herself. But – she did not know how. She had simply not covered all of the subjects that I was being taught at school. Especially the maths! (My mother found modern mathematics very challenging.) To this day I am moved when she recalls how she would cry because she wasn't able to help me do my mathematics homework. So, with the support of my father, she made the very hard decision to resign from her well-paid job as a catering manager and begin a three-year teacher's training course to become a teacher – all just in order to teach me. I have never heard of another mother who has made such a sacrifice for her son.

Becoming a student again was not easy for a grown-up woman in those days. Student teachers were obliged to wear school uniforms, and I remember my amazement when I saw my mother going off to school in a school uniform. To make matters worse, teachers' colleges were boarding schools. So – I only saw her on some of the weekends! During term time Dad then became both dad and mum to me. Even today, when I think of how my mum was willing to humble herself in this regard, because of her great love to me, it still gives me goose bumps.

During those years of her studies, she made very, very sure that I also focused on my studies. Over the weekends and after her graduation she slowly helped me to get back on track.

In doing so, my mum quite literally saved my entire future life – and made possible everything that has happened to me since. I learned so much from her. Not only my mathematics tables, but by her example. I learned what it is to help a child in need, and also that if you know something needs to be done, then you should never give up. You should persevere. Day by day, each of us builds our character, and we can achieve things if we simply keep going, a day at a time. Those lessons have guided my own life and have given me the courage and determination to achieve things that otherwise would not have been possible.

I recovered my schooling just in time, for when I was about eight, my father's job was transferred once again, this time to the coastal Pwani, Mombasa province. And it was shortly before this that I went through the rite of passage that turns every Mbeere boy into a man: circumcision.

Irua

Irua is the Mbeere term for circumcision. According to my

Mbeere culture, boys were usually circumcised at the age of 12 to 15 years. (Girls also underwent FGM, which thankfully today has been outlawed, because it is cruel mutilation, and very harmful.)

I had grown up being told stories of what awaited me. When I was a small boy one of my uncles, Meru, would tell me gruesome stories about how he and his friends had undergone the traditional circumcision ceremony of our tribe. It involved, among other things, being chased by the older boys in the tribe, mocked, punctured with thorns, made to jump into a cold river, and being held down. One knife was then used on up to 50 boys at a time! To me, all this sounded like horror from stone age times, and I was terrified. But Meru, my uncle, used to solemnly insist that this is what it took to be a real Mbeere man, and so I tried to face the future with courage.

But my dad had been exposed to the West through his education, and it had made him rethink some of the practices of his tribe, especially the Irua. In addition, his Christian values had also impacted on his views of the whole Mambura ceremony, which was deeply associated to tribal beliefs and practices. So, when my father judged I was ready, he took me to the hospital. There I was treated by a doctor in a white coat, with the benefit of anaesthesia and sterilised instruments.

While I was somewhat disappointed to have missed the drama of the tribal ritual, I was very glad that my father had saved me from a violent process for which I was not fully prepared. After all, we had not been living in the bush like many of the Mbeere, but instead in towns, and our mindset was therefore less intensely tribal, and instead more urban.

Pwani Mombasa

After that, it was time for the next phase in my life. We moved down to the coast, to Pwani Mombasa. Although only eight years of age, I now saw myself as a young adult, and began to take much more responsibility for my schoolwork. I was enrolled in the Matuga

Primary School, in Kwale District. My mother Priscilla was also in the school – but this time as one of the qualified teachers. By now it was easy for her to encourage and help me, even in maths. She was such a good teacher and so loved by pupils in the school that she realised she had found her vocation, and so she carried on teaching for many years, until they appointed her as a Schools Inspector!

Mombasa is a bustling ancient city in Kenya's coastal province, and that move was a great blessing on my life, for it not only opened my horizons on life, but I became fluent in Kiswahili, which I use frequently today. I was also exposed to the Islamic faith, which is the main religion of the coastal province, and which is, of course, a growing influence across Africa today.

My most vivid memory of Mombasa was the day that I got lost in the city. My uncle Stephen from upcountry was visiting us, and my mum took him to town. My three sisters and I went along for the fun. We visited Fort Jesus, built around the 14th century by the Portuguese. What an enormous building it appeared! – and still does. Then my mother led us on into the maze of streets that made up the old city, built by the Arabs, dating from the 15th century.

At this point, I made a disastrous decision. I wanted some sweets, and I had a few little coins that I had saved. I selfishly reasoned that if I announced my sweets purchase to the family, then there wouldn't be enough to go around! So I lingered a few steps behind my family, and then darted into a little shop to buy some. So far so good, but when I emerged from the shop munching my sweets, my mum and the rest were nowhere to be seen! I panicked and began running along the street. Being the old city, the streets were narrow and very crowded. I ran faster and faster, desperate to find my mum and sisters. But soon I was completely lost, a small boy among hundreds of indifferent strangers. Fears of being lost forever, and even kidnapped and possibly made a slave - Mombasa was well acquainted with slavery - filled my mind.

After many moments of panic, suddenly I had a brilliant idea. To get home from Mombasa, which is an island, my mother and sisters would have to use the Likoni ferry to the mainland. So – I would go to the ferry! A bored policeman pointed out the direction, and I began running.

Upon reaching the ferry, I providentially saw a Land Rover from my father's workplace - Matuga District Development Centre – right there on the ferry. What a relief! They gave me a lift and I arrived home just as the sun was setting, so glad to see my dad. I walked in as a champion and told him that the rest of the group were still coming, minus the inconvenient details of how I had lost them.

Meanwhile, my mother, who had to carry Elizabeth, my youngest sister, on her back, together with my uncle and my two older sisters, Lillian and Rachel, had been having a terrible time. Upon realising they had lost me in the street, their sightseeing tour was abandoned, and they retraced their steps to where they had seen me last. They searched shop after shop to no avail.

Desperate, they decided to report my being lost to the nearest police station. The police, rather than comforting my now sobbing mother, only ridiculed her for losing a child. They reminded her that the dangers were very real: I could well have been kidnapped and taken to the Middle East, or enslaved right there in Kenya. It was now quite dark, and having given up all hope of finding me, they headed for home, desolate and heartbroken. Lillian and Rachel wept inconsolably.

By now, my dad was very worried at my mother's delayed return, for I was posing as if it was them who had got lost, not me. He went to the office and requested use of the workplace Land Rover to go search for them.

He met them somewhere on the road coming home from the harbour. What a joy it was to be reunited! Yet by now I was full of remorse for having put my loving mother through this frightening ordeal. My uncle was furious - this was his first-ever visit to Mombasa, and my thoughtlessness had ruined it for him. My parents disciplined me for having run off like that, but secretly I have always suspected that my dad was also very proud that at such a young age, I had had the wit to get myself home again.

All in all, the afternoon had been terrifying. But at least it had left me with a lesson which I have often shared as an adult: that we can get lost from our family and God when we thoughtlessly pursue some selfish, self-centred interest of our own.

Christianity

As well as a love of education, there was another foundation upon which my parents built our family life: Christianity.

Both my father Eustace and my mother, Priscilla, were what is known as 'first generation' Christians. They both came from families who were animists, depending on charms and amulets to help them cope with the many threats and problems of life.

Indeed, one of my great-uncles, on my father's side, had been the village witchdoctor. He had used all sorts of charms and spells and amulets to try and ward off evil and to influence people. My great-grandmother also used charms and spells, because there was so much to be frightened of in life, and she wanted to protect her family.

But when my father was still a teenager in the tiny village of Kanyuambora, in Embu District, one day a Kenyan Christian convert had simply walked into the village on foot and began telling people stories of Jesus. He said that Jesus was the Son of God, and all powerful, but that He was also good. This Jesus did not have to be placated, like powerful spirits, but could instead be approached, because He loved people. This was amazing news!

My father listened with great interest and wanted to know more. But he found it very difficult to contact other Christians: in those days of the late 1940s and early 1950s, Mbeere land was remote, undeveloped and far from civilisation. The only church was a three-day journey by foot. Not even the preacher made it there very often! So, you could walk for three days to find nothing but the odd cow wandering about. As for getting baptised, that was even harder - you had to go a much longer distance, and then the people at that church charged you a precious coin (money) to get baptised. The coin was meant to be in some sense an indication of your commitment. It was all very discouraging.

Yet one day my teenage dad and his uncle decided to set off on the long journey for baptism. Upon arrival, they learned that the contribution coin had been increased to two coins! My dad sweet-talked his uncle into giving him his coin so that he could be baptised, in the hope they would go back home and earn more from farm labouring and come back for his uncle's baptism! Sadly, my dad tells the story that instead, his uncle was so discouraged by this added cost, on top of the frustration of having to pay anything to be baptised that, while he would later go to church, he always refused to be baptised.

In contrast, my mother Priscilla had grown up in the Kamba tribe's village of Makutano, in Machakos County. It was an area that had been regularly visited by early missionaries from the Africa Inland Mission. So my mother grew up hearing stories about Jesus and learning what it meant to be a Christian. I should explain that in our part of Kenya in the 1960s, there was no resistance to Christianity. In fact, becoming a Christian was seen as something that meant you were learned and smart, and more 'advanced' than the other folk. Christians were looked up to and admired. So, little wonder that my mother's parents had also welcomed Christianity and became Christians along with my mother.

My father was greatly encouraged in his young faith by my mother. With her sharing more of the Bible with him, his faith had moved from a simple "I am a Christian because I was baptised" to become a personal commitment to Jesus Christ. In later years, my parents were even able to lead my father's parents away from traditional ancestral worship and witchcraft to Christianity.

All this meant that, as the Mbogo family, dad and mum raised us as Christians. Throughout our childhood, all five of us children were taken to church each Sunday. We sat obediently through many, many hours of fervent preaching and exuberant singing. We were Christians, so of course that was what we did. I never dreamed of rebelling in any way, and I accepted whatever they said about God and Jesus as being true. I formed in my mind the idea that Christians were expected to be good, and that if we were, that was pleasing to God.

But, living in Kenya, I was also always aware of other, darker, spiritual powers around us. Many people practised various forms of witchcraft, and the threat of it was taken very seriously. For example, my grandmother warned us children that we must be careful, or some neighbour might use poison or charms against us. There was a certain mango tree on one of my great-uncle's farm that stood only 20 metres from our village house. We were warned to avoid it at all costs. A spell had been put on that tree and the evidence was there by the pieces of grass that were tied all around the branches. So while we ate mangoes, as was the custom, from all the other neighbours' trees, we stayed away from the mangoes on the bad tree. None of us dared to even touch the fruit that had fallen on the ground. That was the real forbidden fruit!

At the time, my grand-uncle who had put the charm on the tree was a heavy drinker and somewhat violent man. We all feared him. Amazingly enough, in later years he become a Christian and is today a really committed member of his local Anglican parish church!

St Peter's Ishiara

After two happy years in Mombasa, at Matuga Primary School, I had progressed until I was now at the very top of the class. What a tribute to my mother's dedication to helping me, as at my previous school I had been at the very bottom of the class. But now I was 10 years old and it was time to move on. My parents enrolled me in an excellent Roman Catholic boarding school back in our rural tribal region of Mbeere: St Peter's Primary School of Ishiara. It was far away from Mombasa, but my parents firmly believed that boarding school was the best way for preparing youngsters for the exams they would need for high school.

Before I left for St Peter's, my father decided that I should be baptised at the local Pentecostal Assemblies of God Church in Mombasa. The arrangement was that each baptismal candidate had to get into the pool, repeat the Lord's Prayer out loud, take the baptismal vows, and then be baptised.

Well, on the day itself I was very nervous. The thought of praying the Lord's Prayer on my own, out in front of everyone in church, gave me stage-fright, and I could scarcely repeat the well-known words. Then too, the thought of taking solemn vows to an almighty God to whom I had not fully pledged personal allegiance terrified me.

While my father as a teenager had walked for three days in order to be baptised, I would have walked for three days NOT to be baptised! Yet when my moment finally came, I had an unexpected reprieve: upon my stepping into the baptismal pool and standing right before him, the preacher announced that we were running very short of time, and so decided to drop the vows and prayer, and just baptise me, then and there.

My relief was profound! After that, I enjoyed my baptism. I was happy to see my parents' smiling faces, but I was even happier that I had not had to pray out loud or make scary vows. Obscurely, I reasoned to myself that this meant 'I am free to go and live my life – I have not promised God anything.'

Soon after that, my parents packed me up and proudly sent me off to St Peter's Primary School in Ishiara, Eastern Province, Mbeere district, near my father's home village. My mother had tears of pride in her eyes as she said goodbye: her firstborn son had made it to one of the leading boarding schools in the region! In Ishiara the school made me welcome, the other boys were cheerful and noisy, and I settled in very happily. I will never forget that first day. I stayed awake throughout most of the night, revelling in the adventure of having left home and family to take this first step towards independence. I wondered what the future could possibly have in store for me.

School term began, and of course much of the routine was familiar: in addition to regular lessons, study and games, there was regular prayers and worship, though the daily Mass at the school assembly was new to me. I found that most of my fellow pupils had at least some background of Christianity, though I had probably been more exposed to it than most.

But I was 10, and at an age when it was time to discover myself. Instead, I discovered that, while growing up with parents who were Christians had many advantages, it had one big disadvantage, too: everyone just assumed that I would be a Christian as well. It never crossed anyone's mind that I needed to have a choice in the matter.

I could hardly understand my own growing discomfort. I could not have told you what it was that I wanted to change. I never once wanted to be an animist or an atheist, and of course I wanted to please my parents. I was not against God at all. It was just that I was waking up to the fact that I was living a role that had been given to me, and which I had not specifically chosen. My 'will' was waking up, and I had had no chance to exercise it in this most fundamental part of my life.

Yet I did not rebel. I loved my parents, I liked the school, I wanted to do well. So, as the days went by, I found myself living up to my reputation as being a good boy, one who was trustworthy and responsible. I figured that this was the best, and only way forward, and must be what being a Christian meant: that if you did the good things that everyone expected you to do, and that when you died one day, God would say, 'well done'.

And it worked! Everybody at St Peter's thought that I was a Christian, and a good one. In fact, I was so well behaved that they soon made me the school's shop-keeper. They trusted me with all the money because they thought I was the most trustworthy boy in school. They did not know that I was not that faithful, because whenever I sold anything and the student buyer gave me money, I would slip a few of their coins into a little piggybank (in Kiswahili 'potea- literally means lost') I hid in the shop.

Everyone trusted me, but I was deceiving them. Even worse, I felt proud of myself for my success in deceiving them! I considered myself very clever to have fooled both the boys and girls and the teachers who trusted me. The boys looked up to me as a role model, and I knew what I was doing was wrong, but I did not care. I was just proud that I looked so good to everyone.

The two years at St Peter's flew by. I loved the school, though some of the Roman Catholic ways of worship were new to me. For example, in Lent they put ashes on all our heads, which seemed very weird to me. But I was quite attracted by the seeming holiness of much of Roman Catholic worship, so much so that I even began edging my way towards becoming an altar boy. In the end, though, it turned out that I finished at the school before I made it to the altar!

For at 12 years old, it was time for me to take the dreaded exam known as the Certificate of Primary Education (CPE). It was a 'cut off' exam, in that those who did badly were excluded from much further education. But I knew I had worked hard, and so entered the exam with some confidence.

As it was, I attained the full score of A A A, a full 36 maximum points for this exam. When news of my success arrived in Mombasa, how the family celebrated! The 'stupid' boy of Nyeri was gone forever! At 12, I had achieved a perfect academic score, and was headed for Secondary School.

"I blurted out, from my heart, 'I am tired of acting, tired of playing good – let me have Jesus now'."

2
Finding Jesus at Kangaru

'Don't let anyone look down on you because you are young, but set an example for the believers in speech, in conduct, in love, in faith and in purity.' - 1 Timothy 4:12 (NIV)

It was 1980, I was nearly 13, and I felt on top of the world. By achieving a perfect score on my exam for the Certificate of Primary Education (CPE) I had qualified for the top schools. My parents had chosen Kangaru Secondary School, in those days among the leading schools in Eastern Province – and possibly the top ranked. Getting accepted into a school of this calibre had been quite an achievement, and my parents rejoiced with me. Thanks to my mother, gone was the butterfly-brained boy who failed every subject!

Kangaru Secondary School was in the same town where I had been raised as a child, Embu, in Eastern Province (known today as Embu County). The school had been started by missionaries in the 1920s, but by the early 1980s it was a government-owned public school, with a reputation for being especially good at sports. It was to be my home for the next six years.

By now, playing my role as a 'good person' and a 'dependable' student was second nature to me, and I fitted easily into the new school.

It helped, also, that I was naturally good at sports, and very competitive. I was surprised but gratified when gradually fellow students began to notice, and then to admire my ability, and I became popular.

I did not get off to a very auspicious start, however, for I began by choosing hockey. My first weeks on the field were hardly glorious - I was simply trying to survive the arduous process of learning the game!

For there were a number of quite aggressive boys who came from more wealthy homes in urban Nairobi, and who looked down on us lads who had come from more rural schools, where hockey was not much played. I had never so much as picked up a hockey stick before, and so my first few attempts on the field were awkward, and the Nairobi students pressed their advantage hard. They shot the tiny ball in between my feet where I could not control it with the stick, and several of them even aimed the ball straight at my bare legs (I still bear the scars today).

It was painful and humiliating, to be struggling to even hold the stick the right way around, while fending off a flying ball that was being spitefully smashed onto my shins. It would have been very easy to give up on that first afternoon, and try another, less violent sport. But I decided that I would not let them push me off the field so easily. I learned a valuable lesson that day: not to let myself be stopped by 'the jeerers' you meet in life, who mock your efforts and do their best to hinder you. Instead, just keep going and concentrate on your ultimate goal; do not be overwhelmed by the immediate problems at hand.

And indeed, once I had mastered how to hold the stick, and dribble, I began to turn the tables on those lads from Nairobi. For I had one great advantage: I was a very, very fast runner, and I had been trained by an expert: my mother! She, of all people, had competed in running at her secondary school and had made it to the national level. I had inherited her 'running genes', and she had taught me how to use them. So, once I got past the dribblers, and took off down the hockey field with the ball, the boys from Nairobi had a hard time in stopping me!

By the end of the first year our coach, Mr Singh, had noticed me. He was one of those few Asian teachers who had come out to Kenya as a kind of educational missionary, to help boys to learn and achieve good things in our developing school system. He had a keen eye for spotting talent, and a generosity of spirit in wanting to nurture it. Although I was still in a very rudimentary stage of my game, he took me aside one afternoon and declared: "You will become my captain!"

His belief in me, and his desire that I should aim so high, had a galvanising effect on me. I was so elated by his praise that I felt fired up and ready for anything. I believe I would have half killed myself in my efforts to meet his expectations of me. Briefly, I thought back to those teachers who had told me I was good for nothing. Had they any idea of how such negative words could dampen down a child's view of themselves?

As a result of Mr Singh's encouragement, I worked very, very hard - much harder than my urban friends who already knew the game. They could not be bothered to stick to the rigorous discipline of practice, but I certainly could. The result was that I made it on to the school's well-known team in only my second year of playing, and I was then made captain. In our competitions with the other schools that year, we made it all the way to the nationals - beating most if not all of the other teams along the way! With Mr Singh there to guide me, I did indeed stay on and captain the school hockey team for two years. I learned so much from him in the process: about leadership and how to bring out the best in people by affirming their raw talent, and then helping them to develop it.

Serving as hockey captain also taught me a lot about myself. I discovered that I was very much a 'team leader' type of leader. There are various types of leadership, and I was not the dominant sort of leader. Instead, as I really liked people and enjoyed being friendly and approachable, I found that people liked me right back. I soon found myself enjoying a wide range of friends and the social opportunities that the limelight provided. As a teenager, that included, of course, wanting to catch the attention of the girls, and beginning to realise they existed!

Pretending to be a Christian

But as the months of study and sports passed, I also continued to struggle with my inner identity. Who was I, really? I acted as a Christian and a good boy, because that was the role that had been given to me by my parents, and which seemed to just have grown on me over the years.

I went to the school chapel and accompanied my parents to various Christian meetings over the holidays, because it was unthinkable that I should do anything else. I was always reliable and (mostly) trustworthy, because I had always been that way, and my whole public character was based on that.

Many Sundays I did not want to go to church, but could think of no way of avoiding it. Sometimes I wanted to go off and try things like drinking beer, but that would not have been acceptable. So, of course I did not go. The training to outwardly behave like a Christian had been well entrenched!

I felt frustrated and somewhat trapped. To me, being a Christian had become an endless effort to stay within the boundaries of good behaviour. I believed that in order to gain salvation (i.e., an acceptable relationship with God) I had to do all these good works, even though I was bored with many aspects of the role.

Pretending to be what you are not is very hard - I often felt that I was living two lives, and deeply resented it. In later years when I read the English novel about Dr Jekyll and Mr Hyde, I could not only sympathise but see myself well depicted!

As I became an older teenager, I even once or twice thought of running away. Once I had the mad idea of going to India, just because it was the farthest away place that I could think of. In India, I reasoned, since nobody would know me I could just be myself, whoever that was. I had never had the chance to find out!

I was not wildly rebellious – for I really did want to please my parents and my teachers. But all the same, I struggled to always 'tow the line'. My parents and teachers would have been shocked, because on the surface, I was always submissive and obedient. Many of the students would also have been shocked, because increasingly they looked up to me and used me as their role model. All this made me restless and uncomfortable, because I knew I did not deserve such respect.

In this private, confused frustration, I had one friend and ally, whom I shall call John, who was a son of a local pastor. John had also grown up within a fervent Christian family, and he also struggled with the unrelenting 'good behaviour' of our student lives. Having been friends from childhood, we often engaged in little teenage vices in a quest to have some simple fun.

But, whereas I never even got as far as drinking a beer or smoking (which was forbidden), John did start to drink. Soon he was drinking heavily and hanging out with some very doubtful local characters. Shocked, I drew back immediately, but John did not. Within months he had been dismissed from our excellent secondary school. (Sadly, even today I am still trying to get him to stop this drunken way of life.)

Meanwhile, back at school, during this time of restlessness, I was sadly blind to the many people in my church who could have helped me to take that step towards a real faith in God. They were truly sincere in their faith and could have explained a lot of things to me. But I did not go to them, and in the end, it took the most unlikely person imaginable to wake me up to what I was missing.

Eric and the surprise encounter

By now it was 1986 and I was 19. The years had flown by, and it was time to take the scary Form 4 Kenya National Secondary School exam. This was another 'cut off' exam. If you failed to pass it, then you could not proceed to the final two years of High School (known as Advanced, or 'A' levels, and leading to university.)

You bet I was excited when the results came out: I had scored in the top division. My parents nearly burst with pride when they heard the news. My secondary school had a High School section to it, and it was a great joy to find myself going forward, among the 'chosen few', into the 'A' levels section of Kangaru High School.

I had been made a prefect, and this, together with being captain of the hockey team, placed me in a circle of the top student leaders in the school. It was in this circle that I now encountered Eric, another student. Eric played soccer, and was one of the leaders in the game, as well as being a dorm captain. We got to meeting on a regular basis in the evenings, to drink his hot chocolate and talk. Unlike most of us other 'student leaders', Eric came from a well-off family, and was often sent cocoa by his mother. He was a generous guy, and often shared his hot chocolate with us, which made him popular!

Eric had many family advantages, but I could tell that I came from a stronger Christian heritage. Although Eric's family were wealthier than mine, Eric himself was a bit of a rough-looking guy, with wild shaggy hair which in those days meant a 'don't care' attitude. While he was friendly, he was also abrupt, uncertain of himself, and could be abrasive at times.

We were rather unlikely friends, but for some reason we did become friends, and allies as co-prefects. While I looked askance at some of his awkward mannerisms, I admired his generous spirit. He, in turn, could see that I was the more socially adept, and as far as outward appearances went, I became in many ways his role model, especially with regard to the school dress code!

Then came the school holidays, and when we got back to school, I had the shock of my life. As I was settling back into the dorm, Eric charged in on me, upsetting the calm of the room. He informed me he had something important to tell me that would not wait. Intrigued, I followed him outside where we could speak in private.

He turned and faced me with a huge grin all over his face. "Stephen," he announced, "I have become a Christian! I have been born again!"

I looked at him in astonishment, and then even in some irritation. I was his role model. I had been telling him what was good. I was the good guy, he was the guy who was learning from me how to be good. We both knew that. So, what on earth was he thinking of, suddenly turning the tables on me, and telling me this?

And yet, and yet… I could not deny it: Eric had changed. In the days that followed it became clear that he was different. He was more self-controlled, calmer in his manner, even gracious at times. The way he spoke was more dignified, the way he sang – I sat near him in chapel - sounded deeper, more certain than in my case. In fact, at this point I had begun dropping off from attending chapel services. Even the way he clapped his hands during worship was different, and remarkable: it was as if God was right there for him, and he was clapping joyfully and energetically for Him. Eric was still Eric, and yet everything was different. It was perplexing, yet captivating.

I felt then the weakness of my own position. Deep inside me, I knew that I was leading my life as a painted Christian, with everything carefully applied on top, and held there with a lot of effort! Eric's newfound faith was totally different - his Christianity was more like a spring of water, something good welling up within him. He had LIFE; I had rules to follow. I was practising to be a good person and finding it wearisome; Eric had become a good person and was radiant.

Eric challenged me to consider that there might be something he had got that I did not have. I did not like that idea one bit, but as the days went by, I did wonder: was there something more to Christianity that I did not have?

To me, being a Christian had always meant that you acted in a good way. 'Acting good' was a decision that you made each day. But now I was watching Eric closely, and

I marvelled: what had happened to the 'bad' boy who was now 'better' than me? It made me feel so curious.

For as the weeks went by, I could see that above all, there was no strain in his life; he really was enjoying being a Christian. I admired the change in him very much, but simply did not understand it. I did not enjoy being a Christian – it was a constant constraint on me.

'You have to be dead-on perfect'

During the next school break I returned home, still puzzling over Eric's transformation. Then one morning my parents and siblings went up to our village home, leaving me alone in the house. So, I decided to simply put on a recorded tape that I had found on a shelf in our house. (Those were the days when tape recorders were hi-tech!) It was a Christian message of some sort. I sat down and listened carefully. Not that I knew who the speaker was or what he was going to address.

Providentially, the preacher had chosen to talk about how God is perfect. The preacher illustrated his talk by telling the story of a plumber who was trying to fix some pipes one day, when someone who worked in a nuclear station walked by. The plumber boasted about how difficult it was to get all pipes working together perfectly, and how exact the measurements had to be, up to 98 to 99 per cent perfection. Otherwise, the pipes would not meet up, and there would be leaks. The man working in nuclear energy replied that in his line of work, any flaw at all meant certain death. If a nuclear station leaked – even the tiniest weakness or fault in the system would mean total destruction to many. "We have to be dead-on and close the gap perfectly," said the nuclear station man. "We have to reach 100 per cent perfection." The preacher then went on to say that that was what God demands of us: "One hundred per cent perfection".

I sat there alone in my family's house, listening to all this, and my heart was in turmoil. I examined my past life and my present life. I knew that I had been acting well and had been making a real effort to live the high moral life of a Christian. I was doing my best as a self-made moral perfectionist! But to live it 100%? That was simply impossible!

But now – it seemed that that was not the point of Christianity, and that in any case I was doomed to failure. Because the preacher said that on our own, it is simply impossible to please God, because even if we are 99.9 % perfect, we have still failed. The preacher then quoted from Isaiah 64, about how all our good works are no more than filthy rags in God's sight.

I got up and wandered around the room, feeling a wave of anger and resentment and frustration roll over me. I said to myself, "Then all my efforts for the past years have been useless. It is no good trying - He is too demanding - you cannot please Him. It is hopeless, why even bother to try?"

Meanwhile, the tape ran on, and the pastor had begun talking about Jesus. He said that our hopeless condition before God was exactly the reason why Jesus had died. Because we could not meet 100 per cent the standards God expects.

"That was why Jesus chose to go to suffering and let Himself be crucified - in our place -in order to pay for our sins. So that now, in the eyes of God, because of Christ, we can now be dead-on, 100 per cent perfect - just like Jesus. Not because of what we do, but because of what has been merited to us through Christ. We are still weak human beings, but in the eyes of God, we are counted as complete, without sin, in right standing with God!"

When I heard that, my pacing round the room stopped. I stood still, feeling stunned, shaken, and suddenly very excited. At last, for the first time in my life, I really 'got' Christianity. THAT was why it was called Good News! "Oh my, that is what I need!" I blurted out in the stillness of the room. Waves of excitement poured over me. THIS was the way out from all this effort of acting good.

Alone in the house, I blurted out, from my heart: "I am tired of acting, of making a continual effort to be what I am not. I am tired of playing good – let me have Jesus now."

I sank to my knees. I humbled myself and knelt before the living God and asked Jesus to come into my life. And He did. At that moment, I finally became a Christian. This was between just the two of us, Jesus - and me. And I felt transformed. I wept.

Several hours later my dad and mum returned home, and I met them, bouncing, at the door. With great excitement I blurted out what had happened to me. I announced that I had become a Christian!

My dad and mum stared at me in astonishment. Little wonder as, after all, they had thought that I had always been a Christian! But – apparently not. So, they quickly readjusted their thinking, and then shared my delight at what had happened that momentous day.

Early steps at discipleship

Back at school after the break, I eagerly looked out for Eric, and dragged him to one side. "Eric, I now know what you were talking about! I know Jesus! I am not just hanging on to religion anymore! I am changed!"

Eric was thrilled and we became truly great friends for the rest of the two years at Kangaru.

In the weeks that followed, I sometimes thought back with sorrow on all the useless efforts that I had made to 'be' a Christian. I had been carrying so many burdens - of trying to be good, or continually acting out before my parents, who had always taken it for granted that I was a Christian.

In the meantime, Eric and I were enjoying our new-found faith. Soon we were joined by a few other boys in the high school who had also become Christians, and who were as passionate as we were about seeking and growing as disciples of Jesus. One of them, Simon, whom we fondly called Simo, offered to 'disciple' me. I happily agreed.

First of all, Simo decreed that I must read my Bible every day, without fail. I must also start memorising various verses. Simo had been influenced by the Christian youth organisation the Navigators, who always stressed Bible reading and using little Scripture memory cards to memorise the Bible. That all sounded good to me, and so that became part of my new routine: to read something from the Bible each day, and to memorise something from the Bible each day.

Secondly, Simo said we must make time to pray each day. Our school schedules were pretty full, so we decided it would have to be early morning. Simo agreed that he would come and wake me each morning before dawn, well before 5am. This was easier said than done, as we were in dorms at opposite ends of the school, and I was a sound sleeper. But Simo was not to be deterred, and so would creep along through the trees from his Mwea dorm, around the other dorms, until he reached my Gichugu dorm. He would then tiptoe in as silently as he could, and grab my foot, softly whispering, "Steve Steve, wake up. It's time to go pray!"

At first, it was very hard to wake up so early, and some mornings I almost pretended not to hear him. But he would not let go of my foot, and so I finally had to respond. Then we would creep past rows of slumbering boys, go outside into the cold darkness and pray under a tree.

Simo had been well nurtured by Navigators, and he passed on so many good things to me. He taught me to pray with real passion and persistence. He would tell me: "Stephen, prayer is the way for us to have a relationship with Christ. For us to walk with God, we need to have prayer and read His Word."

That made good sense, but at first it was very hard. I really struggled to get up so early, but finally I got used to it. Then came the morning that I even woke up before he grabbed my foot! After that, as the days went by, I 'caught' the routine, and would meet him halfway, as he came from his dorm. I was catching the discipleship bug!

Thirdly, Simo taught me how to fast. The first time I missed a lunch meal I went to the dormitory and lay down. People asked me if I was okay, and I said I was fine, but inside I feared I was dying. I was so hungry! But Simo urged me to keep at it, and gradually I learned the discipline and power of fasting and prayer.

And so, Simo mentored me. It is to him that I owe the rewards of practising the disciplines of the Christian life, which ensured that I grew well in my new faith.

The courage to testify

Of course, as well as Bible reading, prayer, and fasting, there is another aspect to a healthy Christian life: the ability to testify to your faith. Here I encountered a barrier that not even Simo could help me get over. I discovered that I was simply terrified of speaking in public about Jesus. I loved Him, but still was unable to speak about Him.

So in the months that followed, I stayed a sort of 'backbench' Christian in the school's Christian Union. I went to all of the meetings, but always sat at the back, in silence. I knew I should be contributing, but I felt too intimidated. I was sure that if I started to speak, it would end in disaster, in trembling and stammering - and when nervous, I did stutter. This blockage became a big challenge for me. I raged about it within myself. What was wrong with me?! I could lead a hockey team of bold and competitive lads and hold their respect. Now when I wanted to talk about Jesus, who was everything to me, I was overcome with shyness and fear. I felt tied in knots.

Eventually I began crying to the Lord about it. I so badly wanted to talk about Jesus in that Christian Union, where it was common to meet for singing and then have a time of sharing testimonies. At each meeting we students would be invited to share what the Lord had done for us that week, or else share a Scripture verse that had meant something in our recent lives. We called such testimonies 'presentations', but the idea of attempting one myself simply terrified me.

So, at each Christian Union meeting I would sit at the back and listen to the others, and marvel how they spoke with such fluency. I found that I could not even pray in public. When the leaders called for someone to volunteer to pray, I would always slide down in the seat so that they did not pick on me!

What made it even worse was that I had a premonition that God might just be calling me to become a preacher. I don't know how I knew this, but I did. It was awful – how could I ever preach when I was too terrified to say anything at all? I sympathised with Moses and his fear when God called him to public speaking. So I prayed a version of his prayer: "God, I am the wrong guy to be a preacher for you."

Finally, one Saturday, when everyone else was out and about, I crept up to the dorm on my own, got down on my knees between the beds and prayed. Rather, I simply cried my heart out. I continued in this agony for a possible 20 minutes. I was pleading with the Lord to break and remove this fear from me. Suddenly, I felt God's Spirit sweep over me. An unknown language came to my lips and I simply let go and praised Him. Something in me which had been constrained simply relaxed, let go, and broke. I hid down between the beds and prayed and cried out to God, marvelling at what was happening to me. I had never felt the love and presence of God like this before. It was so real!

That same Saturday evening I went along as usual to the student Christian Union, but this time I told the leader, Brother Shariff, that I had something to share. Shariff was astonished - he had tried several times before to get me to speak. Now he half smiled at my request. "Well, okay…" He was very sceptical!

The meeting began, ran its usual course, and then at the very end, Shariff announced, "Now, finally, there is a boy here who told me earlier that he had something to say. So let us hear it." And he glanced my way, looking doubtful.

But I came forward, feeling no fear, just a little trepidation. I wanted to tell the boys what had happened to me that afternoon so badly that I simply plunged into my story. Before, I had always wondered at others' fluency - I thought they must have a small pre-recorded recorder to tell them what to say! Yet now I stood and just blurted out how much God had done for me. "The Lord has poured His Spirit on me this afternoon..." the floodgates had opened, and the words just came, and flowed from me like a tap.

The faces of the boys and girls who listened that evening were a picture of perfect bewilderment. To this day I can see their faces! They were totally astonished; they knew me as the shy boy; but I was not shy now! That evening marked a major turning point for me in my Christian life: my public ministry had begun. But it had also dawned on me from the onset that I had to fully rely on Him. I knew that this wasn't me - it was Him enabling me by His Spirit to share His works in me!

From then on, I never looked back. The constraint had gone. I wanted to speak about Jesus every chance I could get! I am not implying it was always easy. Rather, as I waited on Him in prayer, I would get enabled to speak His word in the various opportunities that came my way.

My first evangelism

Another major step in my early Christian life was my first-ever attempt at evangelism. It also happened at Kangaru High School, during my last year.

I was part of a small prayer group of Christian boys that prayed regularly for the non-Christian boys in the high school. We asked God to show us how best to reach them with the Gospel.

Then one night I had a vivid dream. A group of people had died and were rising from the dead. In order to enter heaven, they had to stand before Christ and explain to Him why they should be allowed into heaven. One was saying he was a philosopher, and another one that he was a really good person, and the other one that it was because of the blood of Christ.

Next morning, I kept thinking about the dream. It had given me an idea. I shared my dream with another friend from the prayer group, and we decided to write a drama based on my dream. Then we enlisted the help of other Christian students to perform the drama in front of the entire high school. To our delight, it was well received. The preacher of the day then concluded with sharing the message of Christ, and a number of students made commitments to Jesus! For several weeks after the play, students throughout the school were discussing something they had never thought about before: what reason would they give God to be allowed into heaven one day?

That school play was my first-ever effort at evangelism, and so was very memorable to me. It also showed me the importance of being obedient to a small idea, or prompting, from the Holy Spirit.

Trials and temptations

Meanwhile, the school terms hurried by, busy with study and sports and my Christian activities. There were the usual ups and downs of life. As every Christian discovers, the spiritual life is not led on a continual 'high'. When the first joy wears off, Satan is waiting right there, to try and discourage you. After all, you have run off from his 'jail', or kingdom.

There were temptations, for being a teenage Christian in the late 1980s was hard. It would have been easy to get distracted by all that life seemingly had to offer in this world: discos that the school entertainment committee hosted every term, girls, money, and even smoking, drugs and alcohol. All these were common temptations in my school. In fact, in the few years after my year group had graduated from Kangaru, the high school got a very bad reputation, due to drugs. It got so bad that a teacher even advised my dad not to bring Joseph, my younger brother, there!

Other times, the attacks came not as temptations, but as an open attack on us as Christians. For example, by now Simo and I had started meeting with other lads for prayer in the school assembly hall, very early in the morning. But, alas, our school principal was, for some reason, against prayer! Nevertheless, we persisted, because we reasoned that we were not breaking a school law, as we were not praying during school hours.

Then, early one morning, at about 5am, while we were deep in prayer, the principal suddenly stormed into the hall. It was so unexpected that we nearly jumped out of our skins, and I could feel my heart pounding in fear. He commanded silence and huddled us all together. We were so scared, to be under 'arrest' by none other than the school principal, who was a giant of a man with vast, bulky hands, which he often used to cane students. He was infamous for caning students. (In those days caning was officially used in Kenyan schools.)

First, he demanded to know what we thought we were doing, which was a bit superfluous, as we had obviously been praying. It was customary for each one of us to huddle down and be praying out loud, crying to God. We had been all fired up, with each one of us praying fervently, when he had charged into the room.

Sternly, he ordered us all to come to his office at 8am. Feeling sick, we obeyed. Once there and without allowing us to say anything, he expelled us all from school for a week, following which we were to return with our parents.

What a sad day it was. We packed our things and left school with a heavy heart. How could we explain this to our parents? What a disaster - to be sent home in disgrace for praying! Thankfully, my parents were believers, and in the end, they were okay about it. Even so, I did have a hard time explaining to my dad just how I had managed to get myself expelled for praying! I could see he was shaken and somewhat alarmed by what might happen next, and was wanting to ask me: did you go to school to study or to pray?!

But I felt so concerned for those boys whose parents were not

Christians, and who would be simply furious with them for jeopardising their education in any way. Such parents would not have any understanding or grace towards their sons over wanting to pray.

After the one week of expulsion, we all obediently returned to school. We had to come with our parents to face the school principal, and in those days, school principals had the upper hand over parents. The principal glared at us all, and laid down his conditions: we were to be received back, but if we were ever caught praying again, we would be severely beaten with the cane. We knew he meant it, and it was a terrifying thought.

However, once back in school, and in-spite of that stern threat hanging over us, we found ourselves energised to pray together even much more. Supposedly, that little persecution had only strengthened our faith. No wonder it's said "the blood of martyrs is the seed for the church." Thankfully, we did not get caught again!

'God has forsaken you'

Before I graduated from Kangaru, I was to gain another lesson in how Christians can come under spiritual attack. I was to discover that Satan also attacks us by cleverly planting a lie in our minds. That lie can do so much damage - it deceives, confuses and so weakens us. I discovered that Satan is very good at psychology, and when he knows what your lifeline is, he does his best to cut it.

In my case, it happened one afternoon when our final year class members of the Christian Union were being bid farewell. It was a party and meant to be a joyful occasion as the rest of the Christian Union were 'sending us forth' – as having successfully completed school as believers. Suddenly, from nowhere, this thought came into my head: "God has forsaken you. It is all over between you and God."

The awareness of God's presence in my life was a strong factor and one that I had cherished and cultivated in my walk with Him. However, I had somehow come to rely too much on feeling - the blessings of joy, peace calmness – as the evidence that Jesus was present with me. I was still a very young Christian at the time and did not yet know the Bible verses which would have assured me that the thought of God forsaking me was a ridiculous lie.

Instead, I believed the lie – totally. And sure enough, within seconds I was feeling dejected and empty, convinced the God of peace and calmness was gone! I totally lost my taste for the delicious meal before us and lost attention to what was being said. The last I recall was David Juma, the outgoing Chairman of the Christian Union, giving his farewell remarks based on Paul's remarks in Acts 20. Then my mind totally drifted off into despair.

After the meeting, I left the school building and quickly wandered off behind the dormitory. I felt something terrible had happened, that I had been chastised by God. Fighting the tears, I finally crept into a big overhanging bush where my friends and I would sometimes meet to pray. I wanted to hide from the other boys. I felt desolate. I cried out to God in some panic: "You have forsaken me…."

Then the grace of Jesus fell on me, and I experienced a moment of such blessing and reassurance… He would never leave me. I was comforted and strengthened. I was encouraged and knew from that point onwards that I was not to rely on my feelings when it came to my walk with God. Feelings were too easily influenced by circumstances, and instead, I must learn to test the thoughts that came into my head. I learned the lesson that Satan, as a deceiver and the father of lies (as the Bible calls him), shoots darts of lies into our minds to hurt us and trip us up. He is a liar and wants to destroy us.

And so I reached the final weeks at Kangaru High School, and it was time to sit my 'A' level exams. I had chosen to do Maths, Physics and Chemistry, or, as someone with a sense of humour had called them, the Mad Peoples Combination!

The six years had changed me so much for the good, and I thanked God. I was by now an assured student, with good grades and with many friends. My future was full of good possibilities.

Above all, I had found Jesus Christ for myself, and was continuing to grow. Three daily 'disciplines' kept me on track: prayer, Bible reading and fellowship. Each day I would pray "Lord, strengthen me, make me strong to keep my eyes on you." I wanted to walk with Him daily, in good communion. I wanted the muscles of my mind to be able to resist evil.

Psalm 118 and Psalm 119:8-11 became key verses to guide me. They dealt with how a young man can keep his ways pure… "your word have I hid in my heart, that I might not sin against you." I was determined to store as much of the Bible in my heart as I could, by memorising it.

Finally, fellowship: having friends who were also devout believers was a great strength to me. When I occasionally 'wobbled', they were there to steady me, and of course I did the same for them.

Throughout it all, I was learning to depend on the Holy Spirit in prayer. A Christian only grows through spending time with God in prayer. That was where you got His favour, and where His blessing could be found.

I had already learned to depend on the Holy Spirit with regard to overcoming my shyness in public speaking. Now I was learning to be reliant on the Holy Spirit to give me the words whenever I had an opportunity to talk about Him, as well as learning how to resist the devil and his lies, and to trust the Lord for victory over all the hurdles of life.

Graduation day came, and I left Kangaru High School. The rest of my life lay ahead of me. What would I do with it?

*"Find your own way home!" Dad stormed
off in a cloud of dust*

3
What happens now?

'They were glad when it grew calm, and
He guided them to their desired haven.'
- Psalm 107:30

I graduated from Kangaru High School in late 1987 and went home to hit a blank wall – and trouble.

By now, home was in Nairobi, as my father had changed jobs again. After a government grant which had enabled him to do an MA in Britain, he had moved to lecture at the Kenya Institute of Administration in Kabete (Nairobi's outskirts) where he and mum had schooled in the late 60s and early 70s. After a short stint he was then invited in 1986 to join Daystar University (in Nairobi) as a lecturer. Daystar was in its early stages at that time and was among the few pioneer private and Christian universities. It was smaller than the big government universities in Nairobi, and in those days many students from wealthy families went there.

I was nearly 20 years old, and it was high time for me to plan my next step. My father had approached the subject with me many times already, and my future was becoming a source of real tension between us.

He was keen for me to go on to university and then into a recognised profession. He had worked hard all his life, both academically and professionally, climbing the ladder the hard way. He was now determined that his son should follow his example, inspired by his sacrifice.

Of course, I understood his point of view. I knew that it was only because of my father's achievements that my own childhood had been one of privilege. I had never had to save a penny to pay for my education; my parents had always paid for the boarding schools, and even now they would help me get to university.

But although I greatly admired my father, by now I was an aggressive young Christian wanting to preach, or at least share my faith at every opportunity. Indeed, it had become my passion. My father was a Christian, but also very worried about this growing obsession of mine. He feared that I had become mentally unbalanced in some way, and that I was throwing away a good education.

I should explain that being a preacher in Kenya in those days was not like being one in the USA or the UK. Most of our churches at that time did not offer paid jobs. So being a preacher in Kenya almost always meant having no salary, and no defined job. Some of our friends who had become itinerant 'preachers' had ended up on the streets, struggling to even survive.

My father was most emphatic that that would NOT be my future! His precious first-born son would never become such a preacher!

No word from the University

I agreed with my father that we are called to live responsibly in this world, and to be diligent for Christ. So, although I was passionate about preaching, there was no reason not to go on to university and get good qualifications. But that was the first blank wall that we hit. For, while my results for the 'A' level exams had come through, and I had at least passed all my subjects (though not very well), no invitation to join one of the public universities was forthcoming. In those days the universities sent you an invitation, without you having to apply based on the grades you got. So, January 1988 came - and went - without any invite.

More weeks went by. My father became more and more uneasy. He began to ask: What had I really done at high school? Why was there no university letter forthcoming? Had I been so involved in Christian activities that I had not achieved a good-enough straight entry grade to university? Slowly, he began to feel that that was possibly the case. I also began to worry – had I really let my Christian zeal ruin my studies in the final year?

Such doubts, of course, only become a fertile ground for Satan the deceiver to roll out discouragement and blame!

It all made for a very unhappy beginning to 1988 at our home in Nairobi. However, I engrossed myself in deep prayer and fasting and reading the Bible. This was the only way I knew to remain sane, amidst all the pressure that was mounting. For, adding to my misery, was the fact that I kept hearing good news from many of my former fellow students. Their intake letters had all arrived! They were on their way to various universities!

Being ever an upward-fighter, my dad next made arrangements for me to be interviewed by a leading insurance firm in Nairobi. Dad used the fact that it had been started by Christians to get me interested in going along. It was a long and arduous interview, where the man was obviously trying to assess my suitability for insurance work. The decision came back: they had chosen someone else. Reflecting later on the interview, I realised that I had simply preached to the poor white guy - I can still see the bemused expression on his face! Whatever he thought of my faith, he could see that my heart was not in insurance. And that was true, I simply could not help it.

Yet, this was another failure, and the tension with my father went up a few more degrees. What was I good for? What was wrong with me? I could not get into banking or insurance, and there now looked little hope of university. What was to become of me?

At times you could cut the atmosphere in our home with a knife. By now even my patient mum and four siblings were getting heartily tired of my problems. I felt totally trapped and baffled. I did not want to cause problems for anyone! I had given my best shot at the various opportunities and had relied on God to open some door for my future. But nothing had opened at all – the door to my future seemed jammed tight shut.

Military recruitment

Finally, I heard that the military were recruiting, and the thought came to me - at least I was a strong and good runner. I would become a soldier! At least this was a plan, and so I threw myself into practising for the recruitment. The family could see I was working hard for a goal, and that helped us all calm down a bit.

When I look back on it now, I can only think that I must have been really desperate, because in those days young people with education had no respect for the military. Also, a military career would have left me with no opportunities for preaching. But at the time, I was desperate to get any sort of job!

The day came for the interviews, for which I had to return to Embu. Again, my father was kind, for he drove me the two-hour journey up from Nairobi.

We arrived, and I walked out onto the hot sunny field full of very keyed-up young men. I lined up with them and waved to my father in the distance. For the first time in months I felt a glow of self-confidence. I knew I could beat them, when it came to the running tests. Added to this, I had in my hands a letter from one of Kenya's generals! My father had reached out to one of his old colleagues in the military, now a well-known General at the Army Headquarters in Nairobi (DOD – Department of Defence) who had given a letter of recommendation in support of me. Dad was determined that I should succeed, this time round.

So, I stood in the line, and sighed stifled a sigh at the thought of my future as a military soldier - all dressed up in military fatigues. I knew I would get in, I just hoped that it would work out for me. It didn't make any sense with regard to my passion for preaching, but there was nothing I could do about that. As least I didn't wait long for my turn, since we had arrived very early, and I was therefore at the front of the queue of hundreds of young men.

The first stage of the recruitment process was to present your documents. These included the various educational certificates that proved what level you had attained. With my 'A' level certificates, I would be well ahead of most of the others.

My turn came to hand over my documents to the recruiting officer. I reached into my pocket and out came the letter of recommendation from 'above'. I handed it over to the officer, and yes, he was interested. "Now, your school certificates," he said. I reached back into my pocket for my certificates …and reached…and reached and was soon scrambling desperately in all my pockets. Then the awful, gut-wrenching truth dawned on me: I had somehow managed to leave ALL my certificates at home in Nairobi. Oh my!!!! Here I was, front of the queue, and I had nothing to show proof of even having been to primary school!

The officer said, "I am sorry, young man. Without your school documents you cannot proceed."

It was an horrific moment. The field swam in front of my eyes as I slowly stepped out of the queue. I had blown it. I was disqualified. I felt physically sick – how had I let everything fall apart at this stage, when it had all been mine for the taking? Slowly I began the endless walk over to my father, who was standing at the field's perimeter, waiting for the races, because he was sure I would win them all.

My father saw me coming slowly and could tell something was wrong. He watched with apprehension building as I trudged towards him. I was too shy to look up into his face as I blurted: "Dad, I forgot my certificates in Nairobi."

To say that my father was furious is an understatement! And deservedly so — after weeks of preparation, after he had approached the general for a special letter, and then a drive of more than 100 miles - and it was all for nothing? Another failure? Because I had not even bothered to bring the certificates? He glared at me in total disgust and clenched his teeth. "Find your own way home." With that, he stormed over to his car and drove off in a cloud of dust.

I watched him drive off with shaking knees and a sinking heart. Suddenly I felt very small and lost in the great scheme of things. All the triumphs and achievements of my high school years had come to this - me standing unwanted by anyone in the world, on a crowded field, over a hundred miles from home, with my future a complete blank. I was a complete failure - I had behaved like a brainless, flighty child in forgetting those certificates. Even the military, so to say, had rejected me.

As I lingered around the perimeter and wondering what next, a thought sprang to mind: What about joining the police? Failure can often inspire courage! So, all fired up, I walked from the Embu stadium straight over to the police station. I confidently introduced myself and said I wanted to see the officer-in-charge. The officer-in-charge leaned back on his seat to listen to this overly confident young man. I shared with him my interest to join the police and told him I had completed my 'A' levels at the nearby Kangaru High School.

I did not add that, while at Kangaru School, we students had despised the police for their often corrupt acts, and harshness. I did not add that I knew my friends would be appalled to think I had sunk this low. But I was desperate that day, and the policeman was smiling at me, looking as if he respected me. He was the first person who had looked at me like that in months!

I smiled and relaxed - I had saved the day, and would now be able to return home with some good news. Then: "But there is a problem," he said graciously, and with a fatherly attitude, unlike many often commanding policemen. "You see, we just completed all our recruitment interviews last week. You are a week late. Sorry, son!"

I smiled weakly, and in a daze walked back out into the sunshine. I could not believe it. Even the police had rejected me!

I was so shattered that I could not face going home to Nairobi that day. Instead, I went on to my grandparents' rural home, a short distance away. I think of the young man who, possibly in my position, created his own Scripture verse "It is more blessed to stay with your uncle (I add grandparents) than with your parents." And indeed it was. After a few days of being pampered by my grandparents - I had not given them any details of what had transpired - it was time to go home. They gave me money for the bus-fare for Nairobi, and I could only hope that at home things had cooled down a bit.

I crept into the house quietly, in utter misery and defeat. Upon encountering my parents, my mother, though anxious, gave me that motherly look that says: 'things will work out'. My father would not speak to me, and to me that was good enough. I went to my room and sat on the bed and stared at the wall. I felt abandoned and totally flat. Where was God? I had no idea. There was no sense of God's presence with me now. I tried to pray, but may as well have been speaking to that wall. God felt so distant. I was totally disconsolate.

I had nowhere to go, and nothing to do, and my unhappiness made me restless. I took to roaming outdoors each day, as well as attempting to pray, but that was getting harder and harder. I could not bear to be at home. During the day there was the silent reproach of my mother and siblings. In the evenings, my father came home from work and would barely acknowledge my presence.

Discovering Daystar

One day in around June of 1988, after six months of failing, I was wandering around Nairobi, just to be out of the house. As I walked, I suddenly realised that I had arrived at my dad's place of work, Daystar University. It was a lovely sunny day, and a good few students were sitting outside on the ground. I strolled over to talk to them and asked how they enjoyed university. They told me what an excellent place it was, and how they were enjoying their studies there.

Daystar was a private university, among the first of its kind in Kenya. In those days only the wealthy could afford it. Many rich kids who had failed to get into public university went here instead. However, as I chatted with the students I met outside that day, a thought suddenly burst in my head: Daystar offered a good variety of courses. I asked some more questions and learned, to my amazement, that it offered courses in both the Bible and Communications. Both of them would be ideal for my passion and calling! Why shouldn't I go here? It was a good place, even though the small campus was a far cry from the huge spectacular public universities I had been aiming for. My dad worked here every day – why had he not thought of it for me? Probably the cost.

I stood there on the university grounds in the warm sunshine with tears welling up in my eyes. At last, here was my open door for the future. I was sure God was saying that this was the place for me to study. Of course, the challenges associated with such a venture were huge: mainly the money needed! But I began feeling like David when he felt inspired to take on Goliath. At last I knew the answer to all these miserable weeks of searching, and why every door had been tightly closed to me. It was because this was the university for me, this was where I was meant to be. Waves of relief passed over me: at long last I had a direction. The 'where' was settled. Now all I had to do was to discover the 'how'.

When I approached the subject with my father that evening, he was astonished at my audacious idea. In spite of being a lecturer there, he had never even considered Daystar for me, and with good reason: the cost was prohibitive. Even if we tried, what about my siblings in secondary school? They needed school fees as well! Where was a family like ours going to find the fees for all this education?

My dad had by now cooled down from my army recruitment disaster. So, as I spoke, he listened calmly enough to me. But he was cautious in his reaction and did not get excited at my idea. After all, he had seen too many of my false starts that year! But at least he was careful not to pour cold water on my excitement.

That conversation was the beginning of an important healing between us. After all the tensions, I realised that I had begun to develop a wrong attitude towards my dad. I had become determined that I would somehow succeed without him, to prove to him that I was indeed a man. But seeking to engage with him now, with regard to my going to Daystar, was a way of turning back to him, and humbling myself. After all, he had done more for me than I could ever repay, and he had only ever wanted the best for me.

For the next few weeks our family discussed Daystar more or less non-stop. We began to dream up various ideas as to how we would raise the money. One idea was to hold a fundraising venture that would involve our many relatives and friends.

Then one afternoon my dad arrived home with a huge envelope that had arrived at his place of work. It was addressed to me from Egerton University - one of Kenya's public universities, famous for agriculture and horticulture.

I opened the letter with trepidation. The dates showed the letter had been posted to me way back very early in the year. What was this! The university had offered me a place all along - months ago!

We never quite solved the mystery of the delay. It must have been something to do with my dad's transfer of work and change of address, as I had given his old posting as our address. But why hadn't the Kenya Institute of Administration forwarded it months sooner?

Whatever the reason, the letter's arrival now was both good and bad. On the plus side, my father now knew that I had done well, and that a public university had offered me a place. On the negative side, my father regretted that I was now set on Daystar, rather than a big public university.

But not me. I knew in my heart that I should go to Daystar. Though I did not dare tell him, secretly I saw the delay of the letter as part of the circuitous, tortuous miracle that had guided me there. But there still remained the problem of finance. So, as the days went by, it became a case of 'let's see - if funds come through - Daystar, if not - the public university offer'.

Harambee

As a family we then embarked on what in Kenya is called a 'harambee' - a fundraising drive to raise the money. My parents reached out to everyone whom they thought might be able to help. Harambees are quite common in Kenya and are held for everything from weddings to hospital operations to school fees to funerals.

Well, it was the first harambee that our family had ever attempted, but all our friends and relatives pulled together, and at the end of the day - the miracle happened. We had raised enough funds for me to join Daystar University!

As my family relaxed from the hard push, and were united once again because we had finally sorted out my future, another conversation loomed: what would I actually study, once I got there? I wanted to do Bible but would settle for Communications. But my father was adamant that I should get a qualification that would ensure I would never be without work. "Do business administration!" And so, I did. After all that he had done and endured from me, my dad certainly deserved my complete cooperation.

Send Me To The Nations

My father was so pleased. "This is MY son," he told everyone.

4
Daystar University

'Do not neglect your gift, which was given you through prophecy... Be diligent in these matters; give yourself wholly to them, so that everyone may see your progress.' - 1 Timothy 4:14,15

I began at Daystar at the beginning of the 1989 September (summer) semester, and it was a complete delight, for I soon discovered that there were many Christian students on campus. I suspected that, despite my business studies, there might be many opportunities here for preaching!

My first day on campus, and who did I discover was also here? Simo, my old High School discipleship mentor! He was taking Education and Bible. Simo's dad was an Anglican clergyman in charge of the English Learning School based at the Anglican Guest House. Their home was about three kilometres from Daystar, and so became a place we could disappear to and get a great meal. I also became great friends with Fred Mundia, whose father was a former Mayor of Thika. Fred had a great passion for God's Word and told us when good Bible-teaching conferences were happening downtown. One even had a satellite link to a Christian teaching programme in the USA.

Growing in prayer

Within a few days several of us had bonded into a little team that met for prayer on a regular basis. This included Fred Mundia, Gladys Karoki (now Mrs Obwogi), Janet Weru and Pauline Karanja, all who have become life-long friends. At first, we were able to meet in the little prayer room that was near the library and chapel. It was sound-proofed, and so was a great place of solace, because you could pour out your heart to the Lord, shout or sing, and the people in the adjacent room would not hear a word. We loved it.

Sadly, the university soon needed our prayer room for a classroom, so we retreated into the university toilets to pray, but it got too crowded. We finally ended up over across the road at the Nairobi Hospital, which had an open field. The Catholic nuns prayed on that field by walking around doing laps and using their rosaries. We students lay out on the ground as though resting, but we were praying too. At one point when the field was shut for some reason, we even prayed over at the nearby morgue (Nairobi City Mortuary).

We met each week and we prayed. And prayed. And prayed. In fact, during those early weeks at Daystar, my Christian activity at Daystar was nothing but prayer. Any opportunities to preach never materialised. But praying! Well, at least I could do that, and so our little group prayed as faithfully as we could. We were convinced that 'learning to pray' was the way to our future in the Lord's service, and we believed that we needed training in it, just like in any of the other disciplines at the university.

It was not always easy. I recall at times inwardly asking of God: "Lord why should I pray while others preach?" I wanted to also do the more public work of preaching. But the Lord had other priorities for me. He was training me to realise the importance of prayer. As the weeks went by, I began to see that that regular, persistent prayer, although not a visible public ministry, is actually the most vital part of any effective ministry.

Our little group came to realise that not only must any public preaching be galvanised by prayer, but that we must be content to support the outreaches through prayer, even if we didn't preach at all. We should be content to pray to facilitate others' public ministry and thus, in essence, the advance of God's kingdom.

We picked up and popularised the phrase 'don't organise before agonising!' and 'don't travel before travailing'. For between the prayer and its answer, the saint on his/her knees is being formed!

Learning to preach on the streets

January 1990 arrived, and we began our second term at Daystar. And then, the Lord 'remembered' us! It came about through Johnson Migwi, who was a vibrant believer on campus. When he discovered that some of us new arrivals had a real zeal for prayer and missions, he took action. Johnson began a weekly evening Bible study group that together with the Daystar Evangelistic Team (DET) became the seeds for the Daystar Christian Fellowship (DCF). Johnson would often come looking for us - he was another Simo - indefatigable!

Besides more prayer and discipleship, Johnson soon introduced us to open-air preaching. He took us out onto the streets during the weekends. He had us even preaching on buses. We would get onto a bus and begin singing. That would catch the passengers' attention, and before they knew it, one of us was preaching at the top of our lungs, and making an altar call: asking for all eyes to be closed (but for the driver!), and urging the passengers to raise up their hand if they were saying "yes to Jesus".

It was fairly wild evangelism, but from time to time, a person would indeed respond to our message, tearfully thanking us for ministering to them. To this day whenever I meet with Johnson, we remember those early exploits with a smile: the packed buses swerving through heavy traffic, me clutching the rail with one hand and my Bible with the other, and fervently preaching at the top of my voice all the while!

No doubt about it - Johnson was a real firebrand for the Lord and he energised us. These informal and grabbed opportunities for evangelism certainly helped us to develop courage and boldness. We became shameless ministers, and, like fishermen soon began to discern the right places and times to fish for souls.

It was no surprise to anyone when, in 1991, Johnson was awarded the Evangelist of the Year Award by Daystar University.

Meanwhile, our little group continued to preach on the streets around Nairobi. That sort of outreach works well in Africa. We would take fellow students from campus and then join up with a hosting church on a Sunday afternoon. We would go out into the streets and sing on the street corners. Sometimes we headed over to a rather rough neighbourhood called Kawangware, which lay on the other side of the city. We would set up our little stand on the street and then begin to play the traditional drums, or sing and clap, in order to attract attention.

As soon as a good crowd wandered over to see what was happening, I would start preaching to them, or else act as an interpreter for one of the other students as he preached. Having lived in Mombasa, my Swahili was fluent, and of course I was fluent in English. We preached and prayed with many people. Whenever anyone repented and turned to Jesus, we students were just thrilled.

One day I was preaching to such a street crowd from the verse where St John the Baptist was saying that the axe is laid at the tree, and judgement is coming. A drunk man came forward and said he felt like that cut tree, and he was converted that day. Such results fired me up to keep on going back out onto the streets.

Another time we were preaching in another rough part of the city and had just made the appeal. Among those who came forward was a man who looked very uncomfortable. He demanded: "Is it possible for even me to get saved?"

"Yes, brother," we assured him.

He looked very doubtful. He pointed over at a kind brothel-bar across the road, where the doors were wide open. Inside, men and women were drunk and dancing slowly about. It was a den of poor miserable drunks and prostitutes. The man said: "But - that is my business. I own that place. So, can Jesus really save even me?"

We assured him, "Yes indeed." Then he invited us to his bar, and led us through the weaving, drunken throng. We went upstairs. The contrast of the bleary customers and weary women downstairs, and the neat business-like state of his office was startling.

The man had a business partner who had also heard us preach. They spoke quickly together, and then turned to us and said that they both wanted to pray and surrender to Jesus. They both knelt down and we prayed over them and they shyly gave their lives to Jesus as their Lord and Saviour.

I was still very young, and only a student. I did not know what else to do to help the men, and so I committed them to God, and left it at that.

A year later, while out on another street mission, I realised that I was near the place of the bar. I went to find it, but I could not. I wandered about, asking people where it was. Soon I was told that that business had closed months ago. The Holy Spirit had been at work. To me, a closed den meant one thing: changed men!

Daystar Evangelistic Team

It was during that first year that I also joined the Daystar Evangelistic Team (DET) that went out preaching in a more organised way. This became a great training ground for us all! Our chaplain, the Rev Matthew Mwalwa (now with African Inland Churches) would secure us the loan of the school van, and during the week we would get as far as various local schools for assemblies. When the weekends and holidays came, we would work alongside churches right across the city, and even further away.

Soon I was made the leader of the team, and I felt so very much at home. Over the months we certainly added on the miles. Once we even went as far down the coast as Malindi, nearly 575 kilometres, or more than nine hours away, in order to work with the churches there.

These mission trips taught me a lot about trusting the Lord for finance. Travel costs money, and we students had little enough of that! Some team members would occasionally get help from friends and family, but in my case, this was out of the question. I was adamant on that point: my father's extreme generosity and that of our many family friends had ensured that my university fees were met, but that was all. I was always clear in my mind that my mission trips were NOT something with which I could ever burden my dad. He had enough on his hands, trying to help my four siblings, and also, I thought he would have told me to forget missions, and to concentrate on my studies.

So, I prayed and told God that if I was to go on any mission outreaches, then He was going to have to help provide the finances. This led to some adventures in my life of faith!

One time several of us wanted to go from Daystar (in Nairobi) to preach at some churches that were way down the eastern coast. To get there and back, we needed Ksh 3500 (about 35 USD) to pay for our trip. In the late 80s and early 90s, this was a lot of money for us. But we prayed and prayed - and the exact amount of money was anonymously given to us! It was a great encouragement to our young faith.

Trusting the Lord for my bus travel

Another time a fellow student and I were invited to speak to Machakos Boys High School. Machakos is 63 kilometres southeast of Nairobi, which was too far to walk, and so I would have to find the bus money to go. About a month before that mission to the high school, I began to fast and pray. To get to Daystar every day meant, for me, an hour's walk across Nairobi. So I would use the time to pray two hours a day - one hour on the way to Daystar, and one hour on the way home.

For some reason, my friend had to give up on this trip, but I felt under an obligation to honour the invitation. So, I kept praying for the money I needed for bus fares in order to get there.

The day came to leave, but no money for my trip had arrived. However, I went to the bus stop anyway, and waited. I sensed that God was teaching me to depend on Him, not my parents, because in the future my parents would not be there to help me with money to go wherever the Lord led me to go.

For a while I simply stood at the bus depot, watching the buses coming and going. I even looked round at the ground, wondering if God was to provide by dropping down some miracle money. But no such money dropped from heaven!

Finally, I felt prompted by the Holy Spirit to simply take a step of faith, step out, be courageous and believe. So I prayed, "Okay Lord, the next bus that stops right here in front of me I will believe is the one meant for me." A few moments later a bus stopped in front of me, and so I boarded it. I went all the way to near the back of the bus, to put off the evil moment, because I knew what was coming! I sat down and waited as the bus conductor worked his way down the aisle. He reached me and said: "Young man, where are you going?"

I took a deep breath. "I have no money, but I am going to preach in Machakos." That bus conductor was a rough man, and he did not care at all about my intentions to preach. He began to get cross! Then I had an idea – my mother had made for me an African outfit that was of excellent quality. Sewing clothes for us as we grew up was one of her other ways to make ends meet for the family. I opened my case and showed it to him and offered him that for payment. He looked it over, and then snarled, "No, give me real money or get off this bus."

By now our argument was attracting the attention of the other passengers, including two drunken old men who were sitting right behind me. One of them suddenly shouted in Kikamba, which is the language of my mother, "Didn't you hear what the young man said? He is going to preach! Here, you take this money for him, so that he can go and preach!" And that drunken old man paid my bus fare. When I thanked him with real gratitude, he gave me a bleary lop-sided grin, and promptly fell asleep.

A few hours later I reached the school and was able to preach at a Saturday night service, and then again at the morning worship service on the Sunday morning. The students were very responsive, and I had a wonderful time with them. But then came Sunday lunchtime, time to go home!

The head of the Christian Union was a teacher, and he was very happy with the way my visit had gone. To this day I can visualise him at the car park, shaking my hand, saying, "God bless you, we have been so blessed by your ministry. Travel well." But he offered no money for my bus fare home! I looked at him and thought - if he only knew how I had arrived here.

But, by then I had decided that I was not going to tell him. I knew that if I asked him for money, he would have gladly given it to me, but I felt a check in my spirit. It was as if the Lord was saying to me, "Where I am going to send you in the future, there will be no one to ask for money, so you need to learn to trust Me..."

So instead, we parted on good terms, and I forced a cheerful 'plastic' goodbye smile, and then walked back down to the highway and watched the buses fly past. I felt the enemy close in around me, challenging me. "You are all alone, far from home, with no money. What are you going to do now? You are in big trouble!"

I had two options: to walk or get on a bus. But this time I did not feel any prompting to get on a bus, and so I thought, "Well, here goes, I have 63 kilometres to walk back to Nairobi!" And so - I just began walking. As I walked, I could hear the devil saying to me, "Do you really want to be a preacher all your life? This is what you will be doing!" It was an ugly taunt, and so I responded with defiance. I began to run, carrying my small briefcase with me. Whenever I felt discouraged along that long, long road home, I would run until it left me. Then I would slow to a walk. When the discouragement came back, I would run.

63 kilometres is about 39 miles, and I walked for about six hours, until it began to get dark, and I could see in the distance the very beginnings of Nairobi - the airport lay about 10 kilometres in front of me. I knew that now I was going to be in real danger. It would be dark soon, and there were many gangs of robbers that attacked people at night. They could be very violent. So, should I stop the next bus and pray that the bus conductor would help me, or keep going?

I prayed and decided that at least a bus driver was unlikely to knife me! So, in faith, I flagged down the next bus that came along. It was a minibus, and as I stepped on board, sure enough, the conductor was at the door waiting for me. I said: "I have been preaching in Machakos, and am now going home to Nairobi. I have no money. Will you carry me?" He looked at me, hesitated only a second, and nodded: "Young man, let's go." I then handed him a wheel spanner I had found along the road, and he smiled. Then I made my way to a much-needed seat!

So I got back safely to Nairobi. I thought a lot about the whole experience and realised that God had used that weekend to train me in perseverance. It was important not to give up, and that whatever it takes, you just push back discouragement and keep going.

There are times in life when there is no music, no joy, nothing but discouragement. But still - you keep crawling forward, and you never give up. Home sweet home is still ahead!

My Chapel debut

Chapel services in Daystar were one of my weekly highlights. We had Professor Talitwala, our Principal (today would be Vice Chancellor or University President), who often deeply inspired us with his sermons.

Then, one day, in 1991, our chaplain, the Rev Matthew Mwalwa, informed me that I was going to be the speaker at Chapel one morning. He wasn't requesting me to do it; but simply informing me.

Apprehension seized me. I could not recollect students speaking on that podium! I had not even stood on that podium to share my testimony! How could this be? How could I ever speak in front of the entire faculty and student body?!

Well, the chaplain wasn't waiting for my answer, so I was left to answer my questions myself. It was clear that this was his way of welcoming me into a higher level of leadership, given that by then I had assumed leadership of the Daystar Evangelistic Team. But my ministry and speaking had always been more like a rag-tag minister! Open airs, schools and buses were my ideal hunting grounds for ministry. Yet here I was, now being thrown to the 'top cream'! I shuddered.

I did not inform my dad, nor even my friends, that this big challenge had been thrown to me. I was in that state of trepidation where you just hope that on the given day there will be no chapel at all, due to a low turnout or something. But, in the meantime I was learning to resort to prayer and not let any fear paralyse me. So I shared it with my closest prayer companions, but no one else knew what was coming!

For the next two months I prayed and fasted to prepare for that meeting in the chapel. Finally, the day came. As usual, the chapel was filled to capacity. In fact, we were no longer even meeting at our college chapel, because we had had such a growth in our student body that we could no longer all fit in. We had moved down to the nearby

Nairobi Baptist Church on Ngong Road, and that day the sanctuary was filled with the great and the good of the university.

After the usual singing and worship, the chaplain then summoned me forward. With trepidation, or, as St Paul said, 'with fear and trembling' (1 Corinthians 2) I made my way forward and climbed the steps to the stage. A multitude of faces stretched out before me. I took a deep breath and began. Once past the niceties, I was off on full flight! I could sense the same power that had been with me on that first day that I had spoken in public back at the Christian Union meeting in high school – a wave of God's enabling presence. It carried me along and urged me upwards!

It is said that preaching is a lot like flying - the take-off direction is critical, you have to know where you are going, and you have to know when to land - don't keep circling! So, I took off, and having filled my time with what I wanted to say, I was quickly done. After the service, the chaplain, members of faculty and fellow students surged round me with kind words of thanks. As I began walking out of the chapel, I felt a firm hand laid on my shoulder, so I turned around. There stood my dad, looking all emotional! During my talk I had not noticed him in the congregation, but now he took hold of my hand and began congratulating me - I could see that he had been totally astonished that I had been asked to preach, and he was deeply moved.

We began walking outside together, and he did not let go of my hand. That was the first time, besides our in-house family devotions, that he had ever heard me speak in public, and he looked rather overwhelmed. He was obviously amazed at the liberty of speech that the Lord had granted me, for in my youth I had been rather shy, and had even developed a bit of a stutter at one point. I felt such joy that day - I was so glad that he could see at last what the Lord was doing in me.

My most exciting moments were on the walk back to campus from the church. My dad clung firmly to my hand and kept greeting those we met with a proud introduction: "This is my son." It was fun and a real moment of affirmation from my dad. To this day I see his smiling face, letting everyone know, "this is my son."

Dad then led me all the way back to his office, where we sat while he gave thanks to the Lord for my sermon. As he was himself an accomplished public speaker, who also preached at Daystar, it meant so much to me to have his praise now. Especially after all the turmoil we had gone through before I came to Daystar! Looking back to that moment, I see it as the day when God affirmed my calling to my dad. At last my dad could make sense of all the determination I had shown to become a preacher. His fears as to what might happen to me were being calmed, as he saw that this vocation was indeed God-given.

The smiling shoes

Besides preaching, there were other spiritual lessons to learn, and one of them involved my shoes. As my parents' house was in Ngara, about an hour's walk from Daystar, and I was a day-schooler, I was often walking two hours a day (unless my dad happened to be driving down at the same time). As I owned only one pair of shoes, they were important to me.

But, inevitably, there came a time when they began to wear out. I desperately needed a new pair of shoes. What should I do? I believed that the Lord was training me to depend on Him, and not to always ask my parents for help. After all, if I was being called into full-time Christian ministry in the future, then my parents would not always be there; only God would.

So, I needed shoes, and I decided to ask God for help with them, not my parents. I prayed and prayed for those shoes. My only pair had soles that were fading into what we called a 'baby's face' i.e. shoes so smoothly worn out at the bottom that you can feel every uneven surface on the pavement.

Days went by, and I began to look into the window of every shoe shop on my way to Daystar. Sometimes I would pray for provision to buy a particular pair. Sometimes I would even go in and try a pair on, all the while silently praying. The assistant would agree with me that the shoes looked very fine on my feet. There was only one problem - I could not produce the money to pay for them. Because I had none.

In one shop there was a pair of fine Italian leather shoes that I especially fancied. I had tried them on and found they fitted perfectly. So, I silently prayed over them, but nothing happened. Meanwhile, the soles of my one pair of worn shoes were getting thinner and thinner, with the many kilometres I was walking each day. Several signs of holes were beginning to appear in them.

Around this time my father went on a trip to Israel with some Christian friends. While he was out there, he bought a pair of shoes. He put them on, but within a couple of days the sole began peeling off from one of the shoes. It looked like a smiling shoe! So he tucked them away in his suitcase, and continued using his old pair of good shoes. When he got home to Nairobi, he put the shoes up on a shelf and forgot about them. Some days later I was at home one afternoon and my father suddenly remembered that the shoes were there. "Stephen, could you use some shoes? Why not have these – they will fit you."

I was astonished. I had not even known he had bought the shoes! "Are you sure?" I stammered. I had never dreamed of this happening!

"Yes, yes, of course - I don't need them. You have them." And he handed me the box. Cautiously I opened it, wondering what was coming. To my amazement and total delight, they were the same make of Italian leather shoes that I had been admiring in the shop! I had prayed and prayed for the ones in the shoe shop, and here was the same pair, waiting for me at home! All they needed was some glue to put the flapping, 'smiling' sole back in place!

My smiling shoe needed only a bit of glue!

So, I had my shoes, and there was a lesson to be learned here. I thought about it deeply, realising that I had got off balance again with regard to my father. In my desire to 'grow up' and be independent, I had been trying to push my independence from my father just too far. The Lord had checked me in this. "He is still your dad, and loves you, and I can still use him to provide your needs." So, there was no need to be insistent on complete independence from my parents; God would provide in various ways for me, as He saw fit.

It came to remind me of the two different ways in which Jesus sent out His disciples in the Gospel of Luke. In Luke chapter 10 the Lord gave them instructions not to carry anything because they were learning to trust His provision. But later, in Luke 22, Jesus instructed them differently: to take a purse, a bag and even a sword! So, the lesson was to trust God, but not to dictate to Him how He should provide for me. My father could also be a means of His provision; hence, the shoes.

Though I valued those shoes greatly, I generally sat fairly lightly to things that I owned. My great compulsion was to preach, and I would do anything to get to places where there was opportunity. Such as the time I had boarded another bus without any money, but still was allowed to make the trip because the conductor fancied my wristwatch.

I gave it to him, and got my ride to the far away church... perfectly happy to lose my watch for the chance to preach that weekend. Preaching had become the most important thing in the world to me.

Attacked by robbers

I learned another lesson: that God can protect us from our own misguided decisions. For one day we had held a Christian conference in Nairobi, and it had been wonderful. I had had an amazing time and had learned a lot about the Bible from the various preachers. Then came the time to go home, which was a good few kilometres away, on the other side of the city.

I should have taken public transport, as it was getting dark, and Nairobi is dangerous at night. But I was on such a spiritual high that I thought: 'There is no fridge where I can preserve all this joy, and if I take a matatu (a public minibus) I will arrive home too soon. Instead, I will sing and walk my way home, to give me time to come back down to planet earth."

I tucked my Bible under my arm and left the Kenyatta International Conference Centre, headed towards our neighbourhood of Ngara. Soon I crossed the Nairobi river and reached the biggest roundabout in Kenya - famed to be one of the biggest in Africa. It was a dark night and a dark part of the city - with no streetlights at all. I carried on walking, but now I felt a great deal more sober, and even quite frightened. With good reason: I glanced behind me and saw two men rapidly following me - one was tall and one was short and stout. The tall one soon caught up with me and began to walk very close besides me. I started talking nervously, telling him that I was a Christian, and had just come from a Christian meeting. I even began to preach to him! Knowing he looked dangerous, I figured at least I would tell him the Gospel before he killed me! He just grunted.

Suddenly he jumped at me, hitting my hand so hard that my watch and Bible at once fell to the ground. I was very frightened. I had heard it said in movies that white men's hair stands on end when they are frightened. Well, I felt that mine was doing the same thing. I thought, "I am going to die here."

Then something inside me prompted me to cry out "JESUS!" The man flinched and looked uncertain. I shouted again: "JESUS!" and jumped towards him. Then I could see that it was now the man's turn to get frightened! Then all my fear fled, and I felt like a lion. I shouted, "In Jesus' name, I rebuke you, spirit of theft!" The tall man was now shaking all over. The shorter stout guy came around from the other side and shouted to his colleague, "His stuff is down - let's take it and go!" But then I turned on him and commanded: "In the name of Jesus, even you, I rebuke you!" Then he began shaking. I kept shouting: "In Jesus' name, I rebuke you!"

By now both men stood transfixed, staring at me with real fear. One of them muttered to the other: "This guy is… a different kind of guy…. This guy is…" And suddenly they both turned, and just took off, literally running!

Still all caught up in this divine moment of protection, and still praising the Lord, I bent down and picked up my watch and Bible. Slowly I resumed my walk and marvelled at what had just happened. It was straight out of Psalm 116:3: 'The cords of death entangled me… I was overcome by distress. Then I called on the name of the Lord: "Lord, save me!"'

From the other side of the huge roundabout I saw a group of people now venturing towards me. "Are you okay? Are you okay?" they were very anxious. "We saw those guys jump on you and we were too afraid to come over… did they hurt you?"

I reassured them and said that God had delivered me. I did not add what I was thinking: "Thank God I did not have to rely on any of you!"

I finally got home. My long walk had not been the peaceful winding-down that I had anticipated! After my encounter with the two would-be robbers, I was on even more of an 'high' than I had been when I left the conference. It was very hard to sleep that night, as I lay in bed and my mind flashed back to that violent encounter. That verse from Nehemiah 8:10 kept sweeping over me: 'The joy of the Lord is your strength'.

'We announced our engagement, to everyone's delight.'

5
"Who do you love most?"

'If a foe were rising against me, I could hide. But it is you, my companion, my close friend, with whom I once enjoyed sweet fellowship at the house of God.' - Psalm 55:12-14

The terms at Daystar flew by, each one only confirming how perfectly right this place was for me. I was surrounded by mature Christian friends and lecturers who both encouraged and stretched my early attempts at evangelism. I was building relationships and a network in ministry that would last throughout my life. I had even discovered that I had an aptitude for Business Administration, which I had never suspected! But I worked very hard on those studies. I was very aware of the sacrifices my family had made to get me to Daystar, and of how blessed I was to have had this opportunity.

In 1991 my third and final year at Daystar began, and I started to pray about finding my life partner. My prayer went like this: "Lord, I ask you to help me find my future bride. While I search for her, please keep me focused on You, and enable me to serve You with integrity. And please do guide me from presumptuously choosing the wrong one."

I had seen too many of my contemporaries ruin their lives by getting into the wrong relationship, or by becoming promiscuous. So I prayed that I would be guarded and guided, and that I would remain faithful to the Lord, and wait for His choice for me.

That autumn I met a girl, whom I will call Doreen. She was also a student at Daystar, and we became good friends. Soon it grew deeper, and she looked like the right one to me. Therefore I had a big decision to make, and quickly. In Kenya in those days (1980s and 90s), among the 'born-again' Christian youth culture, there was no such thing as having a girlfriend. You were either just friends, or you asked them to marry you. Dating or spending much time with a girl only ensued if she had said yes to you, and you were engaged.

So, if any student saw Doreen and me even out walking together on our own more than once or twice, and we had not announced an engagement, they would wonder what I was doing. Yet I could foresee that Doreen and I would be together a lot, because most weekends we were already out on preaching tours to schools and churches with the team.

I wanted my relationship with Doreen to be totally honourable and transparent, because by 1991 I was not just the leader of the Daystar Evangelistic Team, but I had helped to found (and became first chairman of) Daystar Christian Fellowship (DCF), which had quickly become the university's over-arching Christian fellowship. As such, I was responsible for all the Christian activities in the university, and so was well-known. This inevitably meant that my lifestyle and Christian witness were up for scrutiny.

And so I spoke to Doreen, and then called all my friends together. We announced our engagement, to everyone's delight. Over biscuits and soda they congratulated us and prayed for us. After this, we informed my parents and Doreen's sister's family, who acted as her guardians. The families on both sides were glad for us. We became an engaged couple. Any time I was invited to go somewhere to preach, Doreen would go with me, if she possibly could. So the year of 1991 ended on a blissful note: I was engaged, and looking forward to graduation the following year.

'Send me to the Nations'

1992 arrived. I began it with high expectations. I was going to graduate within a very few months. Doreen would graduate the year after, and we would get married!

But meantime, that January I attended a big Christian conference in Nairobi, run by the Fellowship of Christian Unions (FOCUS), Kenya's version of IFES. It was a worldwide Christian student movement, and they worked extensively in Africa. Every three years they held a huge Commissioning Conference, which attracted keen Christian students from all across Kenya. My Daystar Christian Fellowship (DCF) was affiliated with FOCUS, and I knew some of the leaders there well. Two of them, Calisto Odede and Julius Twongyeirwe, had even helped me with the groundwork in setting up DCF. I therefore had a lot of loyalty towards FOCUS and looked forward to this tri-annual missions conference. The conference was run in Kenya's biggest university then - Kenyatta University. It would be an inspiring way to begin my final year in college.

For about five days various well-known world-class Christian speakers such as Ravi Zacharias (originally from Lebanon and resident in USA), and others from different parts of the world addressed us on the importance and priority of missions, and on Christ's command to take the Gospel to the nations. In our case, that meant Africa.

At the final session of the conference, Calisto Odede, the Conference Director, would lead us in a Commissioning Service. He would invite anyone who felt called to go into full-time Christian work of any kind to dedicate their life publicly by coming forward for prayer.

The evening before this final service, I had spent some time praying as I wandered about the grounds of Kenyatta University. I had prayed: "Lord, wherever you send me I will go. Give me the strength, oh Lord, to obey your call, no matter what it takes." Little did I know how that prayerful commitment was going to be tested only a few months later!

The evening that we were to be invited forward to dedicate ourselves, I was seated with my group from Daystar University, which I had led to the conference. We had had the chance to perform a small evangelistic drama, and to sing a song. It was:

> *'Ask of me, and I will give the nations.*
> *As an inheritance for you. As an inheritance for you.*
> *My children, ask of me. And I will give the nations.*
> *As an inheritance for you, ask of me.*
> *Here I am. Send me to the nations. As an ambassador for You,*
> *As an ambassador for you, my Jesus, here I am, send me to the nations.*
> *As an ambassador for you here I am.'*

Little did I know that night just how prophetic that song would turn out to be for me.

All I knew then was that when the 'call to carry the Gospel to the nations' was finally made, I was one of many who stood up and went forward to publicly offer myself to God for full-time Christian work. So, they prayed for us, and commissioned us in Jesus' name. Following that prayer and commission, we were all radiant and energised, ready to go anywhere and all the way for Jesus! This was my send-off; my commissioning!

Something is very wrong

Then Spring of 1992 arrived at Daystar, and it brought disaster for me.

For, with only about two months to go before my graduation, I began to sense that something was wrong between Doreen and me. She had become rather withdrawn from me in her manner, and I felt uneasy. Something was wrong between us, and I had no idea what it could be.

Then I began to wonder if there could possibly be 'someone else' in her life. But that was nonsense, and I must be wrong! I had prayed seriously that my future bride would be settled by the time I graduated, so that I could get on with my ministry and not be distracted! From our engagement onwards, I had considered myself as 'married' in that I was irrevocably committed, and no longer seeking for a marriage partner. So, what was happening here?

But Doreen's remoteness increased, and with final exams fast approaching, I needed to find out the truth. So, one day as I caught up with her right in the middle of the campus car park, I asked her straight out: 'Is there someone else in your life?'

Doreen paused, and said simply, 'Yes'. I stared at her, dumbfounded, as my whole world collapsed around me. I asked her who it was, and she said she would tell me later.

I spent a wretched, anxious day, hoping against hope that somehow all this was a bad joke. But when we met up, she disclosed that it was none other than my missions deputy, my best buddy in all the missions. She had transferred her love to him!

Then I felt totally shattered. Here was the lady I had considered to be the heart of my life, the person I trusted most in the world (outside family) saying she had turned her back on me, in favour of my best friend. It was a double betrayal.

The verse that came to my mind concerning my friend was where Jesus said, "he who shared my bread has turned against me." (John 13:18) In fact, looking back, I knew I had often gone with my buddy to visit Doreen, who lived very near the college. She and her flat-mate had often entertained the two of us to tea and bread! I felt physically sick with the shock of it. It is unbelievably painful when two people whom you consider to be your closest friends, go behind your back and, as in this case, then replace you in their lives!

In the hours and days that followed, I cried out to God many times: "WHY?!" I had been so careful to pray about my engagement, and to take it a step at a time. Still it had ended in disaster. In fact, to make things even worse, this was the most critical time for my studies - the exams were right ahead of us. A wrong move now, and their betrayal of me could cost me my degree. I would be in total disaster.

Having calmed myself, my response to Doreen was simply that I believed that God had given us to each other, and therefore we ought to pray and fast as to what we should do now. In my grief and desire to hold on to her, I even thought, "We will fast until we die or until God speaks and tells her that this is wrong, and that she belongs with me!" I sincerely loved her.

We both agreed to pray. I convinced her, and she tried to convince my buddy, that we should all pray and fast. I am not sure how much the others prayed, but I did. I really loved her, I had bought her presents out of the little money I had - handkerchiefs, a watch, and I had even moved a sack of bed slats all the way from my home to help make her bed much more comfortable at the flat she shared with her friend.

All the good things that I had done for her, to show my regard, the various missions that we had been on together, our visits to her relatives and to my parents, who had liked her so much, these memories all kept flashing through my mind. Having come through so much together, how could we think of parting?

I had done everything honourably - made it so public, both families and the college knowing that she was my future wife. So I prayed and fasted for several days that this would be healed. I pleaded with God that Doreen would come back to me.

After about four to five days of this, I felt the Lord begin to ask me: 'Who do you love most? Me or Doreen?' For by now, rumours were beginning to go around that something was very wrong with the three of us. The tensions between me and my missions deputy were beginning to unsettle and divide the Christian fellowship at the university. This was no way for us Christian 'leaders' of the Union to carry on. But, I loved her and kept pushing away the idea of letting go.

Into the second week, I began to feel convicted that our prayer-fight was now doing actual harm to the Christian community at Daystar. All the while, the Lord's question in my mind – 'Do you love me more than you love Doreen?' was getting louder. So, gradually, I began praying, "Lord – let the love that I have had for Doreen as my future wife begin to change so that I can love her as a blood sister." I wanted to still be able to protectively care about her welfare and happiness.

After praying in this way for a couple of days, I finally was able to pray that God would give me the grace to love and care about her as a father. This, to me, was like Abraham and Isaac in Genesis 24. Letting Doreen go was, to me, like Abraham sacrificing Isaac, saying to God that yes, I did love Him more than I loved Doreen.

Gradually, I was given the grace to let go of her completely. I was then able to forgive her for having turned her back on me. I also came to forgive my deputy, for having stolen her from me. It took time, and a lot of prayer, but I finally found victory, and then I was at peace. Through many tears, my 'Isaac' had been laid on the altar.

Then I invited Doreen and my deputy to a meeting. I said it would be a 'parting ceremony' in the university's temporarily prayer room. Each of us would pray for each other, and I would formally relinquish all claims to her, and release both of them to continue their relationship.

So the day came. My buddy - who had been totally avoiding me, never turned up, but Doreen did. It was a solemn moment, unlike the fanfare of our engagement. But God gave me the serenity to remain calm. Doreen knelt down (I didn't ask her to), following which I prayed for her and blessed her, and formally and audibly broke the ties between us. I then prayed for the two of them, and then left the prayer room. I was still heartbroken, but I felt the Lord had given me a great victory over what would have been a disaster, had I let our tensions escalate.

Another twist to my relationship with Doreen was to follow. For only a few months later, Doreen broke up with my former friend and deputy! She then contacted me, and wanted to come back. I felt the sincerity of her explanation that she had been deceived, but I also felt the Lord restrain me. He said to me: "You walked away, and now, just keep walking." I realised that my heart was no longer open to her. God had other plans for me and for her.

And whatever other relationship my future might one day hold, I knew that first, I just needed time to heal.

(In the end, Doreen got together with someone whom we had both met on one of our joint preaching tours. At one point we lived as close neighbours. Her family and mine are still great friends today. I learned that it is important to part amicably!)

Evangelist of the year

In the meantime, somehow, I got through my final exams, but it was a tough struggle. Graduation itself was a flat affair. I was totally drained with all the final exams and the grief of losing Doreen. A friend later told me that at the ceremony I had had a 'far away' look, as if my mind was not there. Another friend was far more blunt: he told me that I had looked like a zombie. When he found out all that had happened, he said, 'Oh my, now I understand!'

Back at home in the weeks following graduation, I tried to make sense of it all. I had wanted my years at Daystar to be also my preparation for ministry. Well, they had certainly been that! God had taken me through quite an additional curriculum, of sorts. I had learned so much more about evangelism and outreach, and had had the joy of founding and leading the Daystar Christian Fellowship. I had been blessed with the engagement, and then put to the test during the grief of the bust-up, and working out how to deal with it.

Slowly the message sank in that that terrible experience had been a kind of 'final exam' spiritually. I had asked the Lord for preparation and this testing was His way of perfecting my commitment to Him. I had learned that I must put God first, and even be willing to let go of things that I truly loved, if they were taken from me. I needed to respond to such loss with God's grace and lack of bitterness – and trust in Him for my future.

My prayer life had deepened so much during my years at university. God had calmed my heart even in the midst of such a final storm. I felt thankful that the Christian Union, full of young, impressionable Christians, had not been harmed through any feud developing between me and my missions deputy. Instead, by my letting go graciously, the tensions had died down.

And, as a final footnote to my years at Daystar, the Lord had smiled on me at Graduation! For during the graduation ceremony I had been called up and honoured with a trophy for being what the school called 'The University's Evangelist of the Year, 1992.'

I was deeply touched and honoured. My fellow students and I had given up all our weekends and free time, and walked so many miles to take part in so many missions, in addition to our burden of studies. But we had expected no recognition. I bet that is the way it will be in heaven, when we hear the words "well done, good and faithful servant," for things and acts we have done on earth without thought of any reward. Winning that trophy was a soothing send-off for me, following that tough final semester.

'Lord, I would love to serve you across frontiers, across boundaries.'

6
Mission to Moyale – Called to The Frontiers

'But you will receive power when the Holy Spirit comes on you; and you will be my witnesses in Jerusalem, and in all Judea and Samaria, and to the ends of the earth.' - Acts 1:8

In June of 1992, with graduation behind me, I hit the ground running. I was about to leave for one of the toughest and most remote regions of Kenya, high up on the north east border.

I was not going alone, for in my final months at university I had worked hard to mobilise a team of fellow students, from Kenya, Ethiopia and DRC, to come with me. This would be our last chance to do a 'Daystar team mission' together, as we would inevitably go our separate ways now that graduation was over.

After prayer and discussion, we had decided to go to Moyale. It was a market town and administrative centre for the arid northeast region of Kenya. Life was hard for the church there; there were occasional stories of Christians getting beaten up or even stoned.

We knew that Moyale was potentially dangerous, and that we might even be risking our lives. Nevertheless, we were determined to go. Moyale straddled both sides of the Kenyan and Ethiopian border, and we believed that a mission there could be very strategic.

I knew well that Moyale was undoubtedly my most ambitious mission yet. But what I did not realise was that Moyale would also be personally life-changing for me. Coming so soon after the 'Commission' conference, it would become a timely test of my own commitment to missions. For Moyale was like nowhere I had ever been before: so remote, and with a strong Islamic culture. With my team, we would be preaching to totally 'unreached' people, most of whom would never even have heard of the Gospel.

Meanwhile, I approached the Nairobi office of Life Ministry Campus Crusade, as they had staff based up in Isiolo, the town closest to Moyale, and therefore good local knowledge. Wubshet Mengesha, one of their Directors, welcomed the idea of the mission. He even committed to being with us all the way, and to make plans for how we would be hosted in Isiolo, Marsabit and Moyale.

My first big challenge was simply to find enough money for the entire three-week mission trip. In all, we needed Ksh 51,000 (about $500 USD). This was a huge sum for us students in those days, and a big test for our faith. We prayed and fasted, and shared our need with the student community, staff and lecturers. They were generous in their response, but with only about a month to go, we still needed about Ksh 20,000 (about $200 USD). There was a real risk that the mission would have to be called off.

We continued praying. Then, amazingly, I received word that a Christian organisation known as Food for the Hungry, of whom I had never heard, would send us the Ksh 20,000. Food for the Hungry was based at Marsabit, one of our planned stop-over towns on our route to Moyale. We were astonished at their generosity, but they later explained that they had been very excited at the thought of our visit, and after that, they could not imagine us not coming. God's ways are indeed beyond our reckoning. We were on the moon with joy and excitement (only this was all happening amidst my exams and my breakup!).

So, the money was raised. The next big obstacle was the road itself. Today, if you go to Google maps for Kenya, it tells you that you can do the 775 kilometre trip from Nairobi to Moyale in ten hours and seven minutes. Not in those days! We were warned it would take at least two full days travelling non-stop, for the only road back in 1992 was infamous for its potholes, ruts and rocks - and even armed bandits. Very few people ever went to Moyale unless they had good reason to do so. The most common transport then was lorries, where you rode among goats and foodstuff. So, we planned our transport and supplies carefully.

When the day came, we left Nairobi at dawn in a combi van and drove north on paved roads for about seven hours to Isiolo. There we spent a night and were joined by members from the Life Ministry Team for the next phase. Here Wubshet joined us, agreeing to act as my co-leader for the mission. Wubshet had organised two Land Rovers, and at dawn the following morning we piled our cases, money and supplies into them. Only Land Rovers could deal with the road that now lay ahead.

We headed north again, towards Marsabit. It was only about 260 kilometres, but even that distance took the entire day. We bounced along over ruts and rocks and around potholes for many weary hours.

At Marsabit that evening we were glad to be welcomed by our kind sponsors from Food for the Hungry. Fortunately, they even lived up to their name and offered us a substantial supper, which we badly needed. This stop-over had been intended for rest, but instead it grew into a time of spontaneous ministry. The local Christians had heard we were coming and were so delighted that they kept arriving at the guest house to greet us. We were invited to speak at their various local churches, which we did next day. One young man, Aila (now Bishop Aila), acted as my interpreter and has remained a friend to this day. The Ethiopian members of our team had the bonus of being able to contact some Ethiopian refugees in Marsabit. Their prayers encouraged their struggling fellow countrymen beyond words.

That final stretch of road up to Moyale was the toughest that I had ever seen. Much of it was pitted with alarmingly deep holes or covered with rocks, while other sections seemed to have eroded away completely. Huge lorries ferrying goats, cows and people were the main vehicles we saw bouncing and weaving towards us. We realised that we were travelling in luxury!

At one point, we passed what looked like a hyena standing by the road - though maybe it was just a scruffy lion. Soon the bushes, trees and grass of the Kenya that I knew gave out, and we were looking out on a flat, barren and arid landscape, covered with rocks, for as far as the eye could see. But still we drove on and on for many hours, seemingly alone in this vast 'no man's land'.

That road drove me to prayer! Throughout the punishing journey I kept asking God to keep us safe, for we had the inevitable tyre punctures and mechanical breakdowns that spice up these missions. In fact, there is a saying: 'a mission is not complete until you have had a puncture'. But our local partners had drivers familiar with that appalling road, and who'd come prepared for all mechanical adventures! And, best of all, no bandits happened to come along as we were fixing our vehicles.

We finally lurched into Moyale at sunset and slowly crawled out of our Land Rovers. We were sore and stiff and very dusty. Yet we had arrived safely, and we were so grateful to God.

But where on earth had we come to? It looked like the ends of the earth, for Moyale is very arid and semi-desert. It was very hot and everywhere we saw women wearing hijabs and men in long flowing garments.

Our new friends took us to the small Anglican Guest house. It was truly a home from home, and the local believers organised a meal for us. To our relief we found that the food was both edible and familiar – rice!

Next morning, we began very early with prayer, as we would throughout the mission. We were very conscious that in Moyale we were on the religious 'frontline', and we needed grace, discernment and courage. We needed God's power and grace if we were to present Him to these people.

The Anglican minister arrived and found me kneeling down praying, which was my usual position for prayer. He later teased me that I had looked like a Muslim myself. I smiled, but replied seriously enough: "No, but I am truly submitting myself to God, all the same." 'Submission' is of course the meaning of the word 'Islam.'

That first morning, we walked carefully into the Islamic town and eventually found the tiny church, where some local Christians were happy to greet us. Though they spoke the local languages of Borana and Somali, we discovered that they also had Swahili, so that we could at least communicate easily. They were amazed we had come all that way just to see them.

But the meetings were slow in picking up, as the Christians in Moyale seemed almost casual about coming to church. This surprised us, but over a couple of days we kept preaching, both in the church and even (we risked it) in the open market area, and gradually we could see their hearts open to our message. A few weeks before our coming, some believers speaking in this same market had been pelted with stones. We preached, prayed and watched, with all eyes wide open! The local believers were encouraged and emboldened by our faith and courage. Even much older Christians seemed to listen to us – young people as we were. Our having come 'all the way from Nairobi' gave us some authority in their eyes! In those days 'coming from Nairobi' was seen as 'going to Kenya.' They were so removed from Kenya that they saw themselves as living in another country.

Crossing my first frontier

Then came the day that we agreed to venture across the border. So quite literally, I finished preaching in the church on the Kenyan side, walked for about 20 minutes with our guide, and then started preaching in the church on the Ethiopian side. It was both the shortest and longest walk I ever made, for in those very few minutes we entered a totally different culture. The difference astonished us.

Back on the Kenyan side, the people had a basic stone church building and benches. Here on the Ethiopian side the church was no more than a huge, temporary, shade structure. But - and this was what amazed us - there were a lot more people here and many of them seated on the dirt ground! We were told that when news of our forthcoming visit from Nairobi had got out, the Ethiopian Christians had come in from all over the area to meet us. Many had walked for hours to reach that simple structure, and some had arrived nearly half a day early. Now they all sat patiently on the ground, waiting for our arrival.

We were delighted to greet them, because we had wondered what reception we would find from the church on the Ethiopian side of Moyale. The country had only just emerged from years of harsh oppression under a Marxist Socialist regime. President Mengistu Haile Mari had shut the churches and persecuted the Christians. He had fled Ethiopia only the previous year, in 1991, and now the country was slowly opening up again. It was no longer illegal to preach the Gospel and to be a Christian, but how many believers had held on to their faith through those hard years? It seemed, at least in Moyale, that somehow these Christians had survived.

As I preached to these dear brothers and sisters in Christ, who had been through so much suffering, I could see a wave of joy, of hopeful expectation sweep over them. It struck me so hard that these people had been deliberately spiritually starved for years. They were simply famished. They yearned for the Word of God, to hear more and more about the Gospel of Jesus Christ. On many faces, there were even tears running softly down their cheeks as they hung to my every word. My heart went out to them.

And it was then, as I preached with all my might, that a realisation swept over me: the Gospel need of these Ethiopians, and thousands like them, would haunt me. God was showing me the desperate need for Christians to take the Gospel to 'regions beyond', to the unreached peoples of Africa; to people who had had no chance to hear of Jesus Christ. I felt a premonition that this was to be my life's calling.

In talking with the Ethiopians after the service, they confirmed that this was the first time in many years that they had been able to meet openly and listen to the Gospel without fear of being arrested. For some of them, it was the very first time they had heard about Jesus so clearly. No wonder they were so joyful and inspired!

For our part, we discovered that getting such a warm response from a congregation really kicks life into a preacher. No wonder that there is a saying which runs: 'If your pastor's enthusiasm is diminished, the best cure is a "holiday" somewhere on the Gospel frontline!' It is a good antidote not just for pastors, but for any Christian.

The days flew by. The only time we came close to violence was one afternoon down at the market. As we were preaching, some bored young Muslims began throwing little stones at us. We did not react, and fortunately the older folk did not join in, because that would have escalated the attack, and there could have been a riot.

Instead, we preached without fear and with authority: we knew that the Lord was watching over us, as we had claimed His promise in Matthew 28:20, to be with us always – even to the very ends of the earth.

The one-week mission was soon over. We bid our kind hosts, now friends, goodbye, tore ourselves from them and tearfully piled back into the Land Rovers. As we rumbled and lurched along those appalling roads home, I saw a truck go by carrying relief food and other goods with the name 'Frontier Enterprises'. The name 'Frontier Enterprises' caught my eye, and my imagination.

I thought back to those Ethiopians and prayed: 'Lord, I would love to serve you across frontiers, across boundaries.' Suddenly, it seemed that this would be the most amazing thing to do with my life.

Looking back on that moment in later years, I realise that it was a prophetic glimpse of my future. God would indeed send me across many frontiers, many borders, many boundaries - and link me up to an organisation whose name and mission equally resonates: African Enterprise!

Get a real man's job!'

Our little Daystar team, tired and dirty, finally pulled into the car park back at the university. Our adventure was over, and it was time to go home to my parents and daily life. We were to part ways and possibly some of us would never meet again. But we were never to forget how we had stood that final testing mission together!

It was an abrupt return. I was full of passion to preach and dreaming of the next mission, but my dad brought me back to reality and immediately put his foot down. "Enough of missions! Enough of preaching! You have graduated! It is time you got a 'real man's' job!"

My heart sank. Here we were again, my dad and I, back into the familiar disagreements about what my future should be. It was a demoralising and hard landing, after the enthralling intensity of university life, the breakup with Doreen, and then that exhilarating Moyale mission. As the days ticked by, the tension between my father and me escalated.

As I explained before, my father's flat refusal that I should become a full-time preacher had nothing to do with his not believing in Christianity, but everything to do with what he had seen happen to people who became full-time preachers.

In Kenya back then, it was common for many young men to choose to become preachers only because they had failed at school and were not much good for anything else. Being a full-time preacher was therefore seen by many as a backward thing to do, a poor man's job, which could be done by anyone, without any qualifications. Many of these guys preached in the streets (and still do) and ran churches with very little education (and still do).

On the contrary, my father had struggled for so long and for so many years to get his education, and then sacrificed so much in order that I might get a good education. This was the understandable reason why he was so adamant that I should make use of it. "You are the first born, you need to get a good job and give back to the family what you have been given." With the African custom of the first-born's role in supporting the family - his was very understandable!

I did see the sense of what he was saying - I knew that I needed to be responsible, and that it was time to make good use of my education. I had been living at home throughout my university years, and of course it was time to give something back to my parents.

But on the other hand, I was so frustrated, because my whole passion was simply to preach. This to me was 'the real man's job'! And even my limited experience told me it was a 'real tough man's job!'!

However, I agreed to cooperate with my dad, and to look for a good job. As he was an established university lecturer, my dad had a number of good contacts across the city. He did some asking around. World Vision had a large presence in Nairobi, and at one point there was talk of my going there. When it did not work out, though, I was not at all upset. Although relief and development are of course vital, I knew in my heart that my particular core calling was for evangelism. I knew that I would be only frustrated and wasting my time to do anything else.

The weeks passed, and sadly, tensions between my father and I only grew. We would talk deep into the night on various possibilities for jobs and careers, given my degree. It seemed that I could not be the son that he wanted me to be, nor could I muster any enthusiasm for the various job opportunities that he opened up.

Finally, one day things came to a head, and I knew that I had to make a move. So, without warning, I just packed my bag and set out for the bus station. I could not bear to be at home a moment longer.

I bought a ticket back to Isiolo, the transit town about five hours (300 km) north of Nairobi where we had briefly stopped on our way to the Moyale mission. Life Ministry Campus Crusade had a camp there which reached out to the unreached people of northern Kenya. It was a good place for retreat; as it was far too remote for my dad to discover me very quickly!

Retreat to Isiolo

The Christians in Isiolo welcomed me. Ignitius Nyaga, who served with his wife on the staff of Life Ministry, were providentially going home on furlough. They invited me to stay in their house, and help myself to the food in their cupboard, and to have some peace and quiet. I did not tell them my whole story, only that I needed somewhere to stay while I was seeking the Lord about my future. My main intention was to pray and fast and seek God. The fact that they would lend me their house during this time was totally providential, and a prayer answered. It's said that coincidences happen when we pray. And, that they stop happening when we stop praying!

Now safely out of reach of my parents, who had put up with me long enough, I felt able to ring home. I found a public phone booth and managed to get through to my father, to at least let him know that I was safe. Then I quickly cut the phone, giving no further details on my whereabouts. I did not want to have them worrying about me needlessly.

Then for several weeks I struggled with the tensions between what my father wanted of me, and what I believed my heavenly Father wanted of me. I prayed, 'Lord, if I become a preacher, it is the poor man's job that I am taking up. I am going against my dad's wishes as the 'first born' in the family, to get a good job, and help him with the family responsibilities. You are calling me instead to a life of poverty and challenge.' I had seen something of the harshness of life without money already - having gone to numerous missions on foot, because I could not even afford the bus ticket. Was this really the future that God wanted for me? So, my prayer was for guidance, that if this was God's plan for my life, that I would be given strength and wisdom to pursue it.

The quiet Life Ministry compound provided a peaceful environment for prayer. I would also wander out to the bushes that surrounded the place, looking for a secluded spot where I could pray without fear of anyone hearing me. For I was in such turmoil that I wanted to pray aloud, lifting my inner agony to the Lord in loud cries, begging for help as He had done with His heavenly Father when on earth (Hebrews 5:7).

Day after day, week after week, I prayed, fasted and read the Bible. During those long two months of waiting and seeking God, I began to sense that the Lord was saying something quite specific to me. It came through in two phrases.

From the reached, to the unreached.

From the possible to the impossible.

In other words, I began to sense that He was calling me not to evangelise all by myself, but to work within the churches i.e., the reached. I was to mobilise the churches into doing missions - to the unreached. 'From the Reached to the Unreached'.

As for 'from the possible to the impossible', I took that to mean that if I simply got started and used what resources and skills I did have, then He would add to that, and thereby achieve things that at the start would have looked impossible. I then took time to write down all the thoughts that were coming forth in relation to this vision. As I wrote I felt I was writing an answer, a business plan for my dad. This write-up would prove to him that I was not simply a rag-tag preacher, but one that had a vision and plans to achieve it!

However, as I prayed and wrote, this vision emerged as a solemn calling, an enormous one, far beyond my means. I was only a penniless graduate, with exasperated parents waiting for me back home! I could not even convince them as to my calling; how would I convince entire churches that they had to get out there and do missions?

And yet, and yet, I knew that this was what my calling was. So those two months became a time of self-examination before God, of tears and of dedicating myself to God for the future.

It was a time of lying low. Though I was friendly with the local Christians, I preached very little, and kept largely to myself. This was a critical time for me, and I needed to spend it on my own, in the bush, in withdrawal from people so that I could concentrate on God, and pour out all my fears and concerns of an uncertain future.

Provisions

Having clarified the task, I desperately needed to reach an understanding with God about providing for my needs in this poor man's vocation, to which I had now fully resigned myself. At that point I was even playing with the idea that I would not go back to my parents' home, but rather hit the road in villages and townships, preaching as the Lord would lead and provide. On one of those contemplative days the words in Matthew 10:10 spoke to me very strongly. 'Take no bag for the journey or extra shirt or sandals or a staff, for the worker is worth his keep.' I searched out the verse and some versions even said – 'take no wallet'!

In other words, if I stepped out to do God's work in faith, He would see to it that my needs were met. I wrote in my journal and in the margin of my Bible to that text: 'the labourer deserves his Food and Clothing and Housing and Transport.' I envisioned these four items as my most critical needs, in order to fulfil the task laid out before me.

I felt God assuring me that He would never abandon me in my need. He was not a sadist, not a cruel boss nor paymaster; He would take care of those things for my life.

So that verse became strong in my heart. I gained the assurance that I was not called to a life of poverty, but to a life where God would supply my needs. I knew that needs would come my way, but my heart was now prepared for this, right at the outset of my life's work. For the assurance was strong that He does care for His labourers and will not leave them desolate. He is not a God who torments.

This was a real milestone for me in my faith: getting clear in my heart and head that God would always provide. And even where provisions were not immediately forthcoming, the assurance grew within me that I would follow Him even then. That gave me the confidence to move forward, come what may.

I then continued to put in writing my understanding of what the Lord was calling me to do. This was to prove useful later, since I still needed to convince my university lecturer of a dad that what I was going to undertake was serious, thought through and well organised. It was the business plan of a preacher who had been to business school!

Mission to Baragoi

Towards the end of my two-month stay, I was getting restless and lonely. It was time to head for home. But then I heard that FOCUS (organisers of the Nairobi conference where I had been commissioned earlier that year) was holding a mission in a place called Baragoi. This was about 250 kilometres from Isiolo, and further towards the northern frontier. By now I had settled with God on the things that had brought me to my prayer hideout. So, I grabbed my Bible and my bag and caught a bus for the long bumpy, dusty road to Baragoi. Having kind of received my personalised commissioning, I wasn't going to miss out on the nearest action!

As we were driving along one of those rough stretches, one of the passengers asked the driver to stop. Some fellow passengers and I were baffled: where on earth was he going? As far as the eye could see, the landscape was all rocks and sand. But it turned out that this area was home for this man. He was really excited to be back, having been far away in the city.

But I could not see any houses at all. I was told that he was a nomad, and so would just begin walking until eventually he met up with his family. They could be miles away, or several days away, looking for pasture. What a lesson it was for me: home is where your family is - even if they are out in the barren wilderness. And what a sobering reminder: these nomads were yet another 'unreached people': it was more than possible that no one had ever yet taken the Gospel to them!

I finally reached Baragoi and joined the big mission of about 300 students and ex-students. We had about seven busy days of preaching among the Turkana people group, and for me it was like breathing fresh air: this was what I had been born to do.

There was one amazing afternoon when, after preaching in the open market, we asked the people to make a commitment to Jesus. To our astonishment, all the people answering our call suddenly fell on their knees, in surrender, and prayed. To them, the mention of God and the call to surrender to Him demanded a physical surrender. In their worldview, the reverence for God was that high. Many made commitments to the Lord.

However, when next day some of them heard the Gospel again, they again fell on their knees in surrender. We had not come across this phenomenon before and had to explain to them that once they had committed their life to God, they were now part of God's family, and did not need to fall on their knees every time God was mentioned! But to them, the mention of the God of heaven demanded that they go down on their knees!

It was a bit misguided, but their obvious commitment was deeply moving. This was the harvest coming in, and was what God had called me to do. I knew that with every fibre of my being, and it revitalised me.

After the mission, I was offered a lift home to Nairobi in a big Diguna Mission truck. This was providence, as Nairobi was by now hundreds of kilometres away to the south, and I had no money. I gladly took my lift on the truck. It was time to go home and face my dad and mum and siblings, who I must admit, I was really beginning to miss.

'Now I had a clear idea of what God was calling me to do.'

7
African Enterprise

*'He said to them, "Go into all the world
and preach the gospel to all creation."'*
- Mark 16:15

Back in Nairobi, my parents were delighted to see me. "Our lost boy is back!" They had accepted that I needed to get away and reflect on my future life. Now they were very curious to know what I had decided.

It was good to be home with my family again. In the familiar comfort of our living room I explained how, after much prayer, I had written down clearly all that I believed God was calling me to do. I wanted to reassure my dad that I had not done Business

Administration for nothing! I knew all about writing business plans.

This did something towards reassuring my father. At least I was not content to drift aimlessly! Quite the opposite: I had spent so much time thinking about my future plans that now, with my parents as eager listeners, my passion for mission simply poured out of me. For over an hour I spoke with a fluency and conviction that they had not seen before. I was well prepared now, and determined to convince my dad that this was a worthwhile venture, well befitting of my future life.

My fundamental 'pitch' to my dad went something like this:

I believe God has called me to work with churches, to mobilise them to reach out to the unreached. I am to mobilise churches and Christians, as 'the reached' to 'the unreached'. I am to labour from 'the possible', using what we have, to 'the impossible' which will come later. The Lord has assured me He is with me and will supply my needs.

I further reminded my dad that I had already been doing this, in a small way, by initiating and running missions at the university. Now I knew that I was meant to start doing this in a big way, by drawing entire churches into doing missions.

So, my parents listened, and gave me a fair hearing. But they reserved judgement. They could see that I was passionately committed to the idea, but they could not see how it would work out in practise. While I don't think I convinced my dad much, my 'pitch' did earn me some peace. He seemed to call a cease fire on discussing my future, and instead gave me some 'wait and see' time.

FOCUS opens an unexpected door

Meanwhile, I was glad to be back in Nairobi! I welcomed the familiar bustle and noise of the city after the solitude and silence of Isiolo. A couple of days after my return, I decided to visit the offices of FOCUS (Fellowship of Christian Unions in Kenya). Launched in 1973, FOCUS by then comprised dozens of Christian Unions mainly from Public Universities and a number of Kenya's private universities and colleges. In those days FOCUS was still in its Ufungaman House offices, and I eagerly made my way across the city to them. As I was the immediate former and founding chairman of the Daystar Christian Union - called Daystar Christian Fellowship (DCF), I was very familiar with FOCUS and several of the leaders there knew me well. That day I simply wanted to find out how they were progressing and to possibly catch some news of how colleagues from the other universities were doing since we graduated.

I was not alone in my curiosity. I arrived to find that a number of other recent graduates were also visiting that day. As we talked and laughed together, swapping stories, one of the staff members, Dr Peterson Wangome, drew us into a group and asked us to go around and share: "what have you been doing since graduating?"

While he was asking in a spirit of friendliness, at the back of my mind I heard my dad asking that very same question. Not again! I hardly knew whether to stay on or quietly slip away! It seemed that every parent and indeed every adult had only one thing to say to a graduate: "What have you been doing since graduation?" They obviously expected immediate – and spectacular – results from each of us!

The various former students, some of whom I knew well, took it in turns to reply. Some of them were triumphant: they had already found a good job! Others were at the hopeful stage, still looking.

Finally, it was my turn. I felt almost as if I was responding to my dad again, and was therefore a bit on the defensive: I described very simply but clearly and firmly my newly formed missions plan. I shared the vision and plans I had written while in Isiolo, that I wanted to mobilise churches to reach the unreached. I wanted to bring churches and Christians together, and to mobilise them to go and preach. I wanted to get them fired up, to go out and do missions. So, my future ambition was really just to build on what I had already done with the student teams while at college, but in a bigger way. For now, I wanted to work with groups of churches.

As they listened, Dr Peterson Wangome suddenly interrupted me. "Stephen, what you are describing is good, but, well there is a ministry here in Nairobi that does exactly that. It is called African Enterprise (AE), and it is based out at Karen." (A comfortable suburb to the southwest of Nairobi). "So, before you begin your own organisation, why don't you go and check them out? Perhaps you could learn from them, and even if later you started your own agency, you would have benefitted from the experience with them."

I was astonished and intrigued to hear that there was already an agency that shared my vision. I immediately agreed that I should go and visit this African Enterprise in Karen. I had never even heard of them before.

At this point, another FOCUS staff member spoke up; Calisto Odede, who had oversight of the Daystar Christian Fellowship. I had worked closely with him in linking up DCF as an affiliate to FOCUS, and he knew me well. He had responded warmly to what I was saying and urged us to ring AE offices at once.

So, Dr Wangome took me into his office, and there and then telephoned AE. He asked to speak to Gershon Mwiti, the AE Kenyan Team Leader. He simply said: 'There is a young man here who has just graduated and who is passionate for missions. Could you meet him and hear him out?"

There was a murmur at the other end of the phone, and then Dr Wangome replaced the receiver (these were the days of handsets), looked at me and smiled: "Gershon Mwiti wants to meet you. He will be expecting you tomorrow morning."

First visit to African Enterprise

Just like that. It was that fast. It was September 1992, and a totally unknown and wholly unexpected door to the next stage of my life had just swung wide open.

(A couple of years later, I was to learn that Gershon had already actually contacted the FOCUS people himself, asking them if they could recommend a young man who had the initiative, organisational ability and drive to mobilise young people for missions. So, unknown to me, God had already orchestrated my next step, and here He was using what had been an informal conversation with friends to launch me through that door.)

In the meantime, I was consumed with curiosity about this African Enterprise. Very early the following morning I made my way across the chaos of a Nairobi rush hour to Karen, and presented myself at the big house that served as the AE offices in Nairobi.

A secretary showed me to Gershon Mwiti's office, and I knocked at the door. "Yes?" came a commanding voice. I went in. Gershon had been in the uniformed services, serving to the ranks of a commissioner, and was therefore naturally very commanding and quite daunting. I was just a young graduate; never having had any workplace experience. I walked inside, stood by the door, and indicated that I was the young man recommended by FOCUS. He looked me up and down in silence, and finally said: "Young man, do you want to preach?"

"Yes."

"You feel called to preach?"

"Yes."

'Tomorrow I am going to Muranga town to set up a mission there. You will come with me." He then instructed me to be at a certain street near my house at 7am so that he could collect me on his way to the highway out of town. And that was it – he returned to the papers on his desk. The meeting was clearly over. I said, "Thanks, see you tomorrow," but there was no reply. I quietly stepped back into the hallway and shut the door to his office, feeling excited but also very confused.

I had come prepared to share with him my vision about the 'reached to the unreached', but I had been in his office for less than two minutes. No interview had taken place. Instead, I was simply told to go with him on the following day. This was not at all what I had expected, but it was still something, and I was excited. I still had no real idea what AE did; I knew nothing about them at all. Later I was to hazily recall having listened to Gershon speaking during a mission at my high school in 1987– when the AE Embu mission was formed. But, at this point I had no idea at all what an AE mission to Muranga would look like, and it seemed that Gershon did not feel the need to tell me beforehand.

I went back home to report to my parents, who were eager to hear all about the interview. I admitted that there had not been one, but that instead I was joining some preacher to go to Muranga. My father and mother exchanged glances. What were we going to do in Muranga? I had to admit that I had no idea. My father sighed and impatiently asked a few more questions. I had quite a task, convincing my watchful dad that I knew what I was up to - when really, I had no more idea than he did!

First mission with African Enterprise

However, early next morning I was out on the street at the right time, and Gershon pulled up briefly for me to hop in, and we set off. If I had been expecting any more information from him on the way, I did not get it; he had several other men in the car, and I was simply supposed to be on board. However, as I listened in on their conversation, I could not help but become excited: it sounded almost like a military campaign!

As the miles sped by, they were discussing among themselves the final plans of what had obviously been a protracted, year-long planning process. This stage entailed a final review of all the churches, confirmation of who would mobilise the pastors, and through them, thus mobilise the local people. They also reviewed their latest progress on the organisation of the money, the food, and who would 'zone' the city for the mission. They even discussed the printing of the posters, confirmed the final venues, and decided which other meetings would be held, and when and where. There was a lot of planning, but they sounded very upbeat about it, and very sure of themselves.

I listened with increasing amazement and respect. I was very impressed. This was as far from itinerant street preaching as you could possibly get! Itinerant preachers often just wandered along the street until they decided to start speaking. But this? This was careful, professional planning being applied to a city wide mission! I became very excited. This was many notches higher than how we students had ever managed to run our missions. In those days before mobile phones, communication in Africa was not always easy, and so we had always left all the local preparations to the care of the local pastors, and made do with whatever preparation they had made. We had simply rolled up when a mission was due to begin, and then started preaching!

For the first time I could dimly see how all the skills which I had learned in business administration - the meticulous planning that goes into running a business, the financial acumen, and skills in people management, could be applied to running an evangelistic mission. This was evangelism at a level that I had never witnessed, never dreamed of, before. These were serious men, and nothing was going to be left to chance. This sounded like a planned invasion of the Gospel through the mobilisation of the churches. It was exactly like the preview of what the Lord had been showing me over my summer of prayerful contemplation. This was indeed from the 'reached' to the 'unreached', the 'churched' to the 'unchurched'. I was getting very excited!

Muranga is about 73 km, or an hour's drive, north of Nairobi, and all the way I listened with keen interest, even though I also felt in a bit of a limbo. What was my part to be in all of this? I had not yet been hired; I had not even been given an interview; nothing had been discussed at all! And yet here I was, on an AE mission.

We arrived and I watched as the AE team members met and strategized with the pastors and leading Christians of Muranga, who together made up the upcoming mission's steering committee. We then drove back to Nairobi, and in the following days I went into the AEE offices each morning and listened with growing excitement to all the final plans that they were setting in place. Joseph Wamutitu, who was then AE Kenya's missions director, befriended me, and became my indirect mentor. I was greatly encouraged when I learned that he was a graduate from Nairobi University, with a commerce background. So

I was not alone! The Lord had called others like me, who wanted to do missions, but had not yet done formal theological training.

Two weeks later we set off again for Muranga and for the big campaign. To my astonishment, I was assigned a particular section of the town for which I was to be responsible. Of course, the local people, because I came with AE, assumed that I was also an AE mission professional, and that I knew everything!

So, I took a deep breath, and took firm control of my 'station'. I put into action all my training, both in business and in mission. I organised the details of where we would meet for the day, how we would organise both our indoor and outdoor meetings, and how we would help the local Christians pray with those who responded to our message. Many did respond, including even one elder of the local Anglican church who was there to show us the various homes for the door to door house visits. During one of those engagements, as we led someone in a prayer of repentance, he too had quietly prayed and beamingly told us afterwards, "I too prayed the prayer of commitment and made the decision to follow Jesus." What a joy!

So the mission to Muranga ran its course, and we returned to Nairobi. A couple of days later Gershon summoned me back to his office. Again, I got only as far as just inside the doorway. "Young man, how did you find it?"

'This is what I want to do for the rest of my life," I replied simply.

I join African Enterprise

"Good. Young man, you are on the team!" Again, that was that. Our meeting was over. There was no mention of 'you are hired', or work conditions, or of salary or anything. But then, neither was I concerned about a salary. I was just so happy to simply be on the team, whatever my role, and even for no pay! After all, at the back of my mind I still saw preaching as poor man's work.

Gershon may not have been the most meticulous employer when

it came to contracts, but I was later to learn so much from him, as he led us to various city-wide missions. His love for stories in communicating the Gospel was a habit that I picked up from him and to this day, 25 years later, I still use some of the stories and styles that I gleaned from him.

Gershon also instilled in us team members a sense of the need for excellence and punctuality. He always demanded the highest standards from us, and insisted that we pay great attention to detail, and that we always carried a task to completion. God's work was not to be substandard, just because He was a loving, forgiving God.

Gershon may have demanded a lot from us, but in return he gave his utmost best as an example. His disgust for laziness and contempt for any lack of self-discipline was very evident! We would often joke that his military experience had prepared him to become a true soldier of Jesus. But Gershon became a true mentor to me, and also to another young man, John Shikuku, who joined us at AE Kenya in 1993. John and I both had a passion to serve the Lord, but sometimes we lacked a sense of what Christian discipleship really looked like, when carried out on a day-to-day basis. But Gershon was always there, to guide and keep us on the straight and narrow path.

One such time was when we were setting up a mission in the Kibera slums of Nairobi. We were meant to meet with the pastors at a certain church on a Sunday afternoon, but John and I, having been in other churches all morning, arrived just a few minutes late. Gershon was already there, but very few pastors had yet arrived – they were keeping to 'African Time'.

Yet when Gershon saw us walk in late, he gave us a stern dressing-down, right there in the church! He was so irritated that he seemed to turn even a darker shade than normal. He made it clear that our late arrival was totally unacceptable. As hosts we should have been there ahead of time!

We really respected him, and to some extent, as young novices, we feared him, too. Seeing him that angry with us was enough for us both to decide never again! Gershon obviously agreed with the American writer Eric Jerome Dickey, who once wrote: "Early is on time, on time is late, and late is unacceptable!" Gershon was rigorous in training us to be efficient soldiers for Christ.

Those first few weeks at AE I worked very hard in the AE offices, doing my best to help the other team members as they prepared for more missions. I had no idea of what terms I was working for under AE, and so was surprised when, at the end of the month, Janet Mworia the accountant handed me some cash. I had no bank account to be paid via a cheque. Indeed, such notions as bank accounts had not yet crossed my mind - what would a preacher do with a bank account?

I get a salary!

To my surprise, it was Ksh 5000, about 50 dollars! I had not been sure that AE staff got paid at all, and this was far more than I would have expected, even had I even known. After all, until I joined AE, I had had no idea that anyone would pay you for being a preacher. Later, I was to learn about the individual well-wishers and churches from within and without the country who financially and sacrificially supported the ministry of African Enterprise.

Back home, I was glad to be able to show my parents that I had actually been paid for my first month of work with this preaching organisation. My dad and mum were delighted to see the cash - they found it very reassuring that I had really been paid.

Some of their fears for my future began to subside. At least I had joined a 'known' organisation, and at least I was not just wandering around the streets of Nairobi with a loudspeaker and a soapbox. But they were very surprised to learn, as I had done, that there was a Christian organisation that actually paid its staff to preach, and even to do evangelism. They, too, had never imagined such a thing.

Then my father made a further tremendous discovery: it turned out that he not only knew Gershon, but he had worked with him! For at the university my father had been in charge of social and community development programmes, and churches often invited him to speak on this subject. As for Gershon, who ran seminars to train various Christians, he had actually asked my dad for his help in facilitating some of the seminars. What a wonderful moment of serendipity!

When my father connected Gershon to my new work, his attitude began to rapidly improve. He had great respect for Gershon, who was obviously not a 'fly by night' preacher, but a man of substance and one who was well respected. I thanked God for such an incredible God-intended 'coincidence' - that my father had already met my first 'boss', and even liked him!

My dad now began to see that there was a divine hand leading me, when he had feared that I had lost my way and would come to ruin. For my father was a Christian, and the 'faith side of things' had never been the issue. (In fact, in later years, my father went on to become an independent evangelical churches preacher. Eventually he was to found By Grace churches and schools, which grew to around 20 churches. Then he became a bishop for these churches, that stretched from Malindi, Meru, Mbeere (my rural home region) all the way to Western Kenya. He and my mum also went on to support AE Kenya, both financially and also by joining in our missions, which they do to this very day.)

Director of Youth Missions

As the weeks went by that autumn of 1992, I settled in well at AE. I even acquired a job title. By October I was named Director of Youth Missions at African Enterprise, Nairobi. God had blessed me beyond imagination!

I hit the ground running, and soon I was travelling all over Kenya, going into towns and cities, speaking in dozens of local churches. I would engage with pastors and their church elders, encouraging them to see the potential in their young people, and urging them to send their young people to us for training. These meetings taught me quickly how to relate with pastors and church leaders, of all varieties. It was excellent training, for I was to need these skill when serving with churches across the various denominations.

Hundreds of young people responded, and we held many youth programmes all over the country, helping these precious young Christians to grow in the disciplines of their Christian faith, and also to wake-up to the need to do their own missions and to evangelise their own towns.

For example, I was sent to the churches of Mombasa, where I organised specialist training sessions such as ministry to the deaf, to the disabled, and the use of music to reach out to the youth. We then invited the young people from churches across Mombasa to come and learn, and then in turn we helped those young people to go out and evangelise their own city, through open air meetings and through using their new skills.

I was keen to show the young people that to be effective in evangelism, you have to remember that 'one size does not fit all', that you can be more effective if you target certain groupings of people. We conducted similar programmes in Nairobi, using the famous Uhuru park as a good place to gather and equip young people from around the city for missions.

In addition to my youth missions, I was also taken along whenever AE held city-wide missions anywhere in Kenya. My role was to mobilise and lead the youth ministry in the city during the mission. Soon I was also appointed to be the Assistant Missions Director, and so found myself getting into the nuts and bolts of organising and planning missions, and alongside that I was preaching to hundreds of young people all over Kenya. It was hectic, but I knew I was doing what I had been born to do – mobilising the 'reached' to share the Gospel of Christ to the 'unreached'.

'Who is this lady preacher?'

8
The Girl in the Red Jacket

A wife of noble character who can find? She is worth far more than rubies. - Proverbs 31:10

At African Enterprise Kenya the months flew by, but despite all the busyness of work, there was another aspect of my life that needed attention: I was 26 years old, and lonely. In early 1993, I began to pray again for a wife.

I had broken up with Doreen in the Spring of 1992, and it was time for me to find a bride. Again, I prayed: "Show me my bride, so that when I go looking, I am not distracted by lots of girls. I just want to focus on preaching, and not be on the constant lookout for my girl."

The late summer of 1993 arrived, and I was invited along with some other young men my age, to go and preach at a Laikipia Evangelistic Team (LET) youth camp in Laikipia, Kenya, about 250 km north-west of Nairobi. My assignment was to do the morning plenary expositions of the book of Philippians. We all took our turn in speaking, and then, on the final day of the conference, when most of the day sessions were done, one of my friends Peterson Rukenya said, "Let's go for a catch-up walk; a lady is the next speaker." Interesting that the lady had been left until the final session of the day - the tail-end of the conference!

So, we slipped out of the building and set off along a bush path, enjoying the fresh air and a chance to talk informally with each other, away from the conference. But as we walked, I kept thinking about what my friend had just said. A woman? A woman was preaching? What woman? Was there really a woman preacher among us? How had this come about? All I had seen during the conference was us guys – preaching and leading the various sessions. I knew it was very unusual for a woman to be preaching at all, and the more so at this conference, where all other speakers were young men. So I was intrigued. After a few more steps, I slowed down, and stopped. I decided to let my friends go on ahead, and I turned back to go see this curious sight of the only woman, whoever she was, preaching, among men preachers.

A lady preacher?

I returned to the conference centre, and slipped quietly inside, leaning against the back wall of the long hall. Sure enough, there was a woman at the front, and she was young, and she was preaching. She did not see me, but I listened carefully and watched her. She was wearing a bright red jacket (I later learned it was her one nice outfit, and so had become her official public outfit, her trademark, as I would later call it). She was speaking well - actually, she was speaking very well. She was on fire with enthusiasm! My attention was caught: so, here was a preaching woman. Young women preachers were then rare, very rare!

I slipped out of the hall as she concluded and wandered back outside to look for my friends.

There was a room at this conference centre which we (male) preachers had chosen to make our prayer room. We called it 'the powerhouse', and at the end of each morning session, we had been gathering there to pray before going through to lunch. Young people in need sometimes came in, and then we would pray with them as well. That day, as I reached the door of the prayer room before dinner, I saw that the girl in the red jacket had just beaten me into the room, and she was about to pray with some young people in need. So, I joined in with her to pray with the young people.

This is Rosemary

Later in the evening after dinner, I was outside along with the others, enjoying the cool of the evening and the beauty of the huge African moon, when one of the organisers of the conference, a friend called Mary, came over to me, leading the girl in the red jacket. She smiled and introduced us: 'Rosemary, this is Stephen. Stephen, this is Rosemary.' We smiled at each other.

At that moment, another friend, Godfrey Mburu, came by and repeated what she had just said: "Stephen, this is Rosemary. Rosemary, this is Stephen." We smiled again at each other. Godfrey then suddenly blurted out: "Stephen, she is a great person that you should get to know!" (In later years I have always joked with him as having been our match-maker!)

Certainly, at that moment, without warning, something within me clicked. I felt that God was giving me some kind of nudge: "You are to get to know this young lady." But we were surrounded by students in a public place, and it was impossible to say very much. Plus, once slapped twice shy. I was keen not to get hurt again! We chatted briefly, and then went our ways, but she had made a big impression on me, that preaching lady in the bright red jacket.

Conference in Uganda

In those few minutes of conversation I had mentioned that I was going to Kampala, Uganda the following week for a conference. She replied that she, too, was booked to go to Uganda for the conference. She also said that she was a student at Kenyatta University. That caught my attention: a student, and yet out on missions? That had been my life, too, only two years ago! We had hardly even spoken to each other, but already she was getting into my heart in an unusual way. Back in Nairobi, I kept thinking about that young woman preacher in the red jacket.

The following week, as planned, I headed out for the conference on evangelism, which was to be held at the University in Kampala. Uganda is right next to Kenya, and this was my first ever time to cross over the border. What should have been a happy new experience was marred when I changed a good amount of money at the border, and then discovered they had badly cheated me!

At the conference registration hall, I discovered that all of us delegates from Kenya had been accommodated in the same student hall. While still reeling from the shock of losing so much of my money, I looked around and saw someone in a red jacket. It was the Kenyan preacher girl! It was a surprise to discover that she had indeed managed to make it, for college term was on and there was also the sheer cost of the conference. I did not hide it from myself that I was glad to see her again.

During the breaks, I made good use of any natural opportunity that I could find to talk to her, without letting it be seen that I was seeking her out. My attention was now caught, and I was quietly observing her, prayerfully wondering if God really had put our paths to meet in this way. But still I was wary. The hurt and pain from the previous relationship, while to a good amount healed, was still in my memory. I did not want to risk the pain of a second rejection. I knew that for me to step out again, and seek a girl's hand in marriage would be based only upon a very clear signal from the Lord. But I had prayed for clarity when Doreen and I got engaged, so now I was less confident that I could hear God speak in this regard. How could I be sure?

Then, during one of the days at the conference, I saw her walking happily towards me along with one of our Ugandan delegates. The Ugandan brother looked very animated! I was shocked to realise that suddenly, I felt very jealous. It seemed that this Ugandan had made his move before I could make my move. The hunt was kind of on! This would never do, so I crossed the street so that she would not see me. I felt very uneasy: I felt deeply attracted to her, but I was not at all sure how to play it. So, I did not do much of anything. The incident had helped me to realise fully the intentions of my heart, but my mind was saying, "Watch it! She might let you in - and then kick you out!"

Anyway, I was soon back in Nairobi and very busy with work. AE was planning to hold a mission in a very tough slum in Nairobi, which became the Mathare Valley Mission of 1994. To help raise support for it, Mary, the Christian girl who had introduced Rosemary to me at the youth camp, invited me to come and speak to her Christian Union at Kenyatta University. She wanted them to know about AE's ministry to the street children. Mary knew that I was passionate about taking the Gospel into the slums and reaching the street children, and she hoped some of the students would be inspired to come along and help us.

What I did not know was that Mary was not just an acquaintance, but a very close friend of Rosemary's. Mary had told her about the meeting, too, and invited her along.

The meeting that never happened

The night of the meeting arrived, and I turned up at the university to speak for 7pm. What a massive campus it was! With 12,000 students on one site, it was the largest in Kenya at the time. Very different to Daystar! But although the hall, when I finally found it, was enormous, no one was there. Maybe they were keeping African time?

I sat down and waited for something to happen. Nothing happened. I was sure this was the hall where Mary had said the meeting would take place and wondered what to do. In those days there were no mobile phones and Mary did not have a home phone. She had invited me by calling our AE office landline from a public phone booth, and there was no way I could reach her now.

Unbeknownst to me, the meeting had been cancelled, and Mary's message to warn me had not got through to me. And Mary had completely forgotten to tell Rosemary that the meeting was cancelled, so a few minutes later the girl in the red jacket turned up, all alone, as if on an appointment to meet me!

So, the two of us sat together in that big empty hall, patiently waiting for something to happen. We waited and we talked, and it was as if God was giving us another chance just to be together and get better acquainted. I wanted to move the friendship on, but I found it so difficult, I was too careful. Fortunately, Rosemary seemed in no hurry at all to deepen our relationship; she was just content to chat as casual friends. This helped me relax, and so we got better acquainted with each other, without either of us feeling under any pressure. And it was all so natural - after all, we were just waiting together for the meeting that was not going to be, to begin!

What I did not realise was that Rosemary, too, had been badly hurt in a previous relationship. She had noticed me at the youth camp, and liked me, but then she had heard that I had gone to a private university, and that my dad was a lecturer there. At that point, she had decided to back away, as her mum had worked in a pub in one of the Kiambu slums, where she had grown up in abject poverty. Her father had died when she was only eight years old and her mother had died the previous year (1993). So Rosemary felt that she and I were from different worlds, and it was no use pursuing any relationship, as she did not see how two such different backgrounds could ever mix. So, while she had equally felt drawn to me, she did not want to give it false hopes.

But that evening, there was no strain between us. We just sat and shared our testimonies, and our interest in Christian ministry. We had two events behind us already – Laikipia Youth Camp and the Uganda conference. A lot to share! There was nothing personal or affectionate mentioned. Nevertheless, we felt comfortable sitting there chatting alone together, and the fact that no one else showed up did not seem to matter at all. We talked and talked. I learned that she was 22 (four years younger than me), had done a teaching certificate before coming to university to do double maths.

Finally, some student wandered by and asked us what on earth we were doing in the hall. We said we were waiting for the meeting. He said, "Oh that meeting got cancelled!"

We were both shocked that no one told us of the cancellation. At once, Rosemary took me to look for Mary. Mary apologised profusely that her message to cancel had never reached me, and that she had forgotten to tell Rosemary. By now it was quite late in the evening, too late for me to take public transport home across the city. So Mary arranged for one of the Christian Union brothers to take me in for the night. I went to sleep on his couch thinking about Rosemary and marvelling how God had used a cancelled meeting to give me a chance to get to know her better - without any pressure!

Rosemary in the red jacket!

A couple of weeks later, Godfrey Mburu (who had been at the Youth Camp and had said "she is a great person that you should get to know") invited me to go and preach at a kesha (night vigil prayer meeting) in Ndumboini, near Upper Kabete campus, Uthiru, where he was schooling. I agreed, and turned up, only to find that Rosemary in her red jacket had also been invited, as the second preacher!

Then a few weeks after that, I was invited by another old friend from Daystar to speak at an evening meeting, this time in Ngong. In those days, we did a lot of those all-night preach/pray meetings. Throughout the night you sing, worship, pray, and listen to various speakers. I arrived at Ken and Kagendo's home in Kibiku, Ngong, and found to my astonishment that the speaker who was booked to follow me was, once again, Rosemary in the red jacket!

By now I was really intrigued, and seriously wondering if this was not God telling me something. Wherever I went, I seemed to bump into Rosemary of the red jacket! It had to be more than just coincidence. From that point on, I began to have confidence that this might well be from God, and that I should now take the initiative! So I began to be more directly friendly and personal with her, and to let our friendship flourish, which it did.

Another few weeks went by, and I had an AE engagement to preach at a youth camp in a town called Busia. It lay towards the Kenyan/Ugandan border. This time I took matters into my own hands, and purposely invited both Mary and Rosemary to come along with me. A mutual friend, Wallace, escorted us to the bus stop. The manner in which Wallace said goodbye to Mary made me wonder if Wallace didn't have feelings for Mary (they did indeed get married and go on to run Missions of Hope in Kenya). As for me, well, I equally felt emboldened during this mission to take things a notch higher in my relationship with Rosemary. 'Spy time' was over. It was time to make my move!

The mission to young people in Busia went very well. Preaching and ministering alongside Rosemary was just so comfortable and felt so right. I realised that I would be happy to have her company as a co-worker for the rest of my life. So, during the mission I kept praying and watching for the right opportunity to make my interest known to Rosemary. But alas, we were so busy with the young people that we were never on our own, and so the right opportunity did not present itself.

The proposal

Soon we had boarded the bus for the ride back to Nairobi, and I decided that it had to be now or never. But again, it was not easy, especially as I was seated next to Mary, with Rosemary sitting on a separate seat a few rows behind us. The three of us had some good conversation, as Mary and I had shared some ministry together among the youth in Mathare Valley slums, and we were telling Rosemary about it. But this was hardly the stuff of romance! As the bus reached the halfway point on the journey home, I kept wondering how to muster the courage to reach out to Rosemary. How could I ask Mary to excuse me, as I had something to tell Rosemary? It was all very awkward.

But finally, I plucked up courage. I quietly asked Mary if she would very much mind trading seats with Rosemary, so that I can chat some more with her. Mary, ever a gracious soul, was so kind, and joyfully asked Rosemary to come forward. They swapped seats, so that was great. So far, so good!

At least Rosemary was now seated next to me. At first, we just carried on talking about how the mission had been. But the miles were going by, and I knew I had to say something more personal pretty soon. So, in that bus cruising back to Nairobi, I finally came to 'the main item on the agenda'. As the bus rocked and jolted down the road I lowered my voice and said to Rosemary "I want to ask you to prayerfully consider getting married to me?" I spoke softly, as we were sitting surrounded by people. But what a moment it was! My heart was pounding. She had had no idea whatsoever that I was about to ask her such a thing, and I had no idea at all as to her feelings towards me - she was friendly, but no more.

Rosemary glanced quickly up at me, appearing surprised, as well she might have been. I had up to this point (in spite of the numerous unique meetings) let out no hint at all that I was interested in her. But she kept her calm and her poise. She thanked me for my proposal, saying she would certainly pray about it. And with that, the boy in the blue jacket (my trademark in those days) had to be content.

Back in Nairobi, I helped the girls get into their transport for the university, and then I got mine towards Hurlingham, where I then lived, sharing a small home with a friend called Jamo (later Pastor James Maina). I was feeling a bit anxious, as I was not at all sure how I would even get to hear from Rosemary again. How would she contact me to let me know when and where she wanted us to meet, so that she could give me her reply? She lived miles away and had no phone.

I had the office phone at AE, but I was out of the office so much of the time. Besides, girls in those days sometimes kept boys waiting for up to three months before they gave them an answer to their proposal for marriage. It seemed that girls enjoyed keeping the boys in some suspense. Would Rosemary keep me waiting for three months? My heart sank.

The answer

As the first week went by, my anxiety mounted. I was so afraid that I would get a 'No!' from her. Perhaps I should have waited a bit longer. Perhaps I should not have proposed to her in the middle of a bus full of people?

Down at the AE office, every sound of the phone ringing brought me hope that she might be the one on the line. But the waiting continued that entire week - without any call from her. I worried and prayed and prayed and worried, and waited.

Then one day into the second week, Leah our receptionist said there was a call for me. She transferred it through to me and thankfully, it was not a pastor calling to speak about a mission or a fellow evangelist or school inviting me to come and speak. It was Rosemary calling from the public phone booth at the university!

I could feel my heart racing. Was it to be a 'Yes' or a 'No'? But Rosemary did not say either way, and she wasted no time in small talk (was there a queue of people right behind her, waiting for the phone?). All she quickly said was "Please come to my shared room at the university. I am now ready to give you an answer, face to face, and not over the phone."

The joy of hearing her voice was soon swallowed by my anxiety. I had expected to get the answer when she rang me! But now there would be more waiting, and I had to go to her for my answer. For some reason, that scared me. To my mind, bad news was shared face-to-face, and good news was always shared immediately!

But the phone had gone dead, and even if I managed to trace the number, there was no way that I could track her down amongst 12,000 busy students! No one at that end of the phone was going to go hunting for the girl in the red jacket!

So I waited until the day she had chosen finally came. Then I nervously made my way over to Kenyatta University to get my answer. Rosemary had played it so cool with me that I honestly had no idea what her answer would be. But I decided to pluck up enough courage to take a cake along with me. If she said no, I would leave it as a parting gift to her. If she said yes, we could use it to celebrate together!

She cheerfully welcomed me into her shared room in the college. Her roommate was not there, as she had asked her for privacy for a very serious meeting, and the roommate had happily obliged.

We exchanged the niceties quickly, and then I said, "Well, here I am, ready to hear your answer to my proposal. I will respect whatever you say as God's will." I had been seriously praying, much more than I prayed for any sermon I had preached around that season, and had decided it would be better to get an immediate 'no' than to go through the 'yes-no" fiasco of two years before.

But to my wonder and joy, Rosemary said "It's a yes!" She stood there smiling up at me, her eyes shining. Yes! She would marry me! God had answered my prayers for a bride, for a wife that would share my life and ministry with me. Oh, the joy and relief that was mine.

Choosing wisely

I hugged her and said, "my thanks" and in came the word "darling", that was later to define our marriage, as our nickname for each other became simply 'D' for darling. I knew she was the right lady for me. I had taken time, observed her without her being aware I was watching her, and in conversations sought to discern her personality. I had observed her doing what was also my calling, preaching and ministry in general, and knew she had the same heart for evangelism as I did. I had quietly studied her and came to the conclusion that we would get along very well indeed.

I was later to learn she had also, quietly in our various encounters, equally studied me!

She had realised early on that she had feelings for me as well, and that that afternoon on the bus she had wanted to say 'yes' right away, but (she later said to me) Kenyan culture in those days dictated that ladies must take more time, and it would never have done to say 'yes' so quickly. So - she said she would pray about it.

What an exciting, high point this was for us. As we shared the celebratory cake, we each opened up to each other. We shared the sad stories of our former broken engagements. As we listened to each other, and how each of us had been committed to the previous relationship and had done our best to rescue those relationships, we realised that God had permitted them to break, so that we could meet.

We also thanked God for how, in His mercies, He had providentially led us to each other and provided several divine opportunities for us to meet. So, having come to Kenyatta University that day with great apprehension, I left Rosemary with a bounce - I was walking on air, I was so happy! The long wait for my future bride (about 7 months) was now over. I was now engaged to the girl in the red jacket!

'Harare was a great gateway experience for me.'

9
AE Missions Director, Kenya

*'But you, keep your head in all situations,
endure hardship, do the work of an evangelist,
discharge all the duties of your ministry*
- 2 Timothy 4:5

Unfortunately, there was little time for me to enjoy my engagement to Rosemary. Indeed, she must have wondered at times where I had gone! For it was now 1994, and I had suddenly been promoted to become AE Missions Director for all Kenya: a challenging assignment, as I was still only 27.

But the former Missions Director, Joe Wamititu, had left AE in order to do church planting on a full-time basis, and so I had been chosen to follow him. Now my passion for taking the Gospel 'from the reached to the unreached' had come true with a vengeance. Suddenly I was in a job that entailed me meeting and engaging with hundreds of pastors across entire cities and motivating them to do mission. An excellent illustration of taking the 'possible' and attempting the 'impossible'!

I was so busy that I could not even find time to break the wonderful news of my engagement to my own family. For I wanted to properly introduce them to Rosemary, and there was just no time.

Not only was my new job very demanding, but I had landed in it just as a major mission to Zimbabwe, the Harare and Chitungwiza Mission '94 - was about to take off. All of our AE teams across Africa were zeroing in on this big city-wide mission, and our Kenyan team was to join in and help. We were all going to Zimbabwe.

And that meant it was time for yet another 'first' in my life: my first ever time on an aeroplane. I would be flying by myself, as Gershon Mwiti, our national director for Kenya, had other commitments before he could join the mission in Harare.

Gershon drove me to the airport, discussing details of the mission all the way, waited while I checked in, and then left me to it. I followed through the security check and immigration process, and then wandered around airside, looking for my boarding gate. I found it and was just settling down in a seat to relax, when who did I see walking towards me with a beaming smile – but my dad!

How he had managed to persuade the immigration and security officers to let him reach the boarding gate I will never know, but there he was. He explained that as this was my first ever flight, he had wanted to make sure I was all ok with the immigration and departure processes. In essence, he was here to affirm me!

I was deeply moved. Here was proof that my dad, whatever misunderstandings we had once had about my preaching, was still my biggest supporter.

I thought back to the other big moment, when I had given my first ever public sermon at Daystar, and how he had accompanied me around the university afterwards, so obviously proud of me, telling all who wished to listen that "this is my son!" Again, I inwardly thanked God for such a wonderful father. It's the kind of affirmation that a son needs from his father or mentor! By now my dad was not only reconciled to having a preacher for a son, he was very proud, and in total support of my work. And that day he had moved mountains at Nairobi Airport security in his determination to see me off on my first ever flight!

I reached Harare with no problem, and spent some hectic days there, preaching in various venues all over the city. Our team had set up a stack of engagements for us, stretching from early in the morning to late in the evening, including some night revival meetings. My meetings were mainly in open air public places and schools. Our senior leaders, such as Michael Cassidy (AE's founder and International CEO/Team Leader) did the Top Leadership events, spoke to the senior politicians and preached at the mass rallies in the parks.

It was in Harare that I first participated personally in praying for the president of a country. It came about because ministry to the Top Leadership was part of AE's approach. Harare being the capital city of Zimbabwe, we had included as part of our programme for the mission a National Prayer Breakfast. This entailed inviting such guests as the Head of State, members of parliament and top government and business leaders. The President then was Robert Mugabe.

Robert Mugabe

President Mugabe had agreed to come to the Breakfast, but then he said he had a stomach upset. So he had asked Michael Cassidy for prayer. So, our AE delegation accompanied Michael to a side room at the hotel to pray for the President. I was the youngest among this delegation and it was a great honour to be among those surrounding him as we laid hands on him. Our prayers must have been answered with regard to his upset stomach, because in response to Michael's challenge to the leaders of Zimbabwe, the President stood up and spoke for an hour!

Harare was a great gateway experience for me. It was thrilling to finally meet, and then be working alongside top AE evangelists from all across Africa. On one of those days Michael Cassidy was to preach on an open ground in the city at an evening rally. Before he spoke, he suddenly invited me to come up to the platform and share my testimony.

Sensing the audience included many people from tough backgrounds, such as having grown up in the slums, I shared about the time when the thugs had attacked me in Nairobi. I told them about how, in my calling upon the name of Jesus and rebuking the attackers in His name , they had fled. The audience was really taken with this story of my encounter. It became a good precursor to Michael's sermon, for he then told them so much more about how they, too, could know Jesus, the mighty Saviour.

On the following day, there was a team meeting for all the AE team leaders and fellow mission directors from all the various national teams across Africa. Some of them were highly respected, international evangelists in their own rights. These included the heavy-weights of AE at that time: Stephen Lungu (author of 'Out of the Black Shadows') who went on to succeed Michael Cassidy; Dr Edward Muhima (who later became an Anglican Bishop in Uganda) and of course my Kenyan team leader, Gershon Mwiti.

Sharing my story

There were also a number of white team members from AE: David Richardson, Mike Odell, and Ernie Smith

Suddenly, Michael Cassidy announced that before he gave the team devotion, he wanted me to share my story with them all. This caught me totally by surprise, and for a moment I was completely daunted. How could I presume to stand up and address all these heavyweights? I was the youngest by far! Michael saw my dismay, but all the same, nudged me firmly forward. Michael is a born 'mentor', he looks for people's future promise, and then sets them forward in a positive way. So, I stepped up and shared the story of my encounter with the thugs, and how calling on Jesus had given me victory.

Michael's affirmation to me that day was critical, for it gave me the courage to speak, and was also a way of introducing myself to the other team members. The warm response I received from the rest of the AE Team was such an encouragement, as I sought to fit in among them. I was later to learn that that was how big-hearted Michael had also brought Stephen Lungu and Gershon Mwiti, among many others, on-board the AE bandwagon. Like Jesus in John chapter 1, Michael had a wonderful way of calling on people to come along and follow him in evangelism, to reach out and attempt things bigger than they could have imagined would be possible. But with Michael's encouragement, they did follow, and did succeed, and then just kept going! To this day 'Uncle Michael', as the younger team members call him, remains a great friend. I am always bewildered as he keeps reminding me, whenever we talk, that he prays for me every day! What a heritage!

Finally, the mission came to an end, and it was time to board the plane in Harare and head back to Nairobi. As we left the lights of the city twinkling behind us, I reflected on what an experience it had been. The Harare mission had only confirmed to me that this kind of work was what I wanted to do with my life: mobilise the churches for missions, from 'the churched to the unchurched'!

Later that same year of 1994, we had the great 2nd Pan African Christian Leadership Assembly (PACLA II) in Nairobi at Kasarani. It too was a time of tremendous blessing, as we met and prayed for Africa with Christian leaders from across the continent. Some of the friendships and contacts that I made then are still going strong, more than 25 years later.

When Mbeere meets Kikuyu

Meanwhile, never mind the hustle and bustle of missions and mobilising churches; Rosemary and I had another kind of mobilisation to do! We needed to get our families on board and enthusiastic about our engagement and marriage. Having previously introduced Doreen to my family as the lady I was definitely going to marry, it was not going to be easy to say, "Well, now it's definitely Rosemary!"

At the beginning, neither of our families was in the least bit enthusiastic.

My parents greeted the news with dismay. They had nothing at all against Rosemary as a person, and they accepted that she came from a humble background and had indeed been orphaned. What worried them was that she was a Kikuyu.

There were two reasons for this. Firstly, the Kikuyu and Mbeere tribes had clashed during the time of British colonial rule, and there was still a lot of historical bad feeling between them, and more so among the older folk. Secondly, the Kikuyu are the biggest tribe in Kenya and suffer from a kind of stereotype reputation for being proud and ruthless, both in business and in their other dealings with people. So my dad could not believe I was seriously thinking of marrying a Kikuyu woman.

"Are you sure that a woman like that will not rule over you?" he kept asking me. There was a saying in our Mbeere tribe about Kikuyu women: 'She will marry YOU!' In other words, a Kikuyu woman would dominate the marriage. In African culture, this was seen as totally unacceptable, the more so as in our culture it has historically been the man who 'marries', not the woman. Thus, a typical African man will not say 'I am married', but rather 'I have married'!

Soon after this, one of the senior leaders from my parents' church, the bishop, invited me out to a local restaurant. I hadn't a clue as to why he wanted to see me, but I suspected he had heard I was marrying, and thought he might want to help me by offering some financial support. Not so! Instead, I was given a very grave lecture on the probable consequences of marrying outside of my own tribe, and above all, if I married a Kikuyu. The bishop even quoted some Bible verses at me, to back up his sincere concern.

I was really shocked, given that he was a well-known man of God, and a great minister of the Word. But rather than try to argue with him about biblical teaching on us all being created equal, black, white, Mbeere and even Kikuyu, I simply told him that Rosemary was the girl I loved, that she loved me too, and that was the basis of our getting married!

Taking my stand against my dad and the bishop was not an easy thing to do. But, unlike choosing a career, this was one area of my life where the decision had to be mine, and all mine. Yes, I was willing to hear their concerns, but in the end, I was the one that was marrying, and the one who would live with the consequences, for better or for worse.

No more tribalism

So I stood my ground. I was convinced that Rosemary was the woman that God intended me to marry. She had a heart for missions, she was strong, but she was not out to dominate me. I made it clear to both my dad and the bishop that the core unifying factors for Rosemary and I were that we were believers in Jesus, and that we sincerely loved each other. We both felt that it was God's will for us to get married.

I then humbly suggested that African tribalism was far too influential in Christian affairs, and that Christians should instead be taught that what matters is belonging to the Kingdom of God, not belonging to any particular tribe. I even playfully said that if they wanted to talk about tribes, then it could be said that all Christians belonged to the tribe of Judah, and that should override all other tribal divides! My mother, being convinced of my commitment and affection for Rosemary, but not wanting to come between my dad and I, quietly encouraged me to follow my heart.

Meanwhile, Rosemary was also having problems with her family, over marrying me. They did not think that I was worthy of her. This needs an explanation.

Rosemary's early life had been harsh. She had been born and

spent her early years in Kangemi, a sprawling slum on the outskirts of Nairobi. Her father had opened a little shop there for her mother, which made it possible to feed their growing number of children. But then another woman had arrived on the scene, disrupting the relationship between her parents. Further trouble came from her in-laws, who wanted the shop for themselves and who therefore, through false accusations, made life unbearable for Rosemary's mother.

Soon Rosemary's father had turned violent against her mother. So Rosemary's mother decided to flee, before she was killed. She left Kangemi with her four young children and three young nieces and drifted over to another slum in Kiambu, in a valley by a stream near the prisons farm. Far above them on one side were the Asians (kwa-ahidi) and on the other side, the wealthy Africans.

Life in the slums

Life was very difficult in Kiambu for a single woman with young children. The slum, like all others, was full of prostitution, drunkards and all manner of evil goings on. Rosemary's mother managed to find a single room in a row of tiny one-room houses, which was all that she could afford. The room was about ten feet square, and the family of eight moved in. There was one bed, which the children took in turns to share with the mother. Otherwise they slept on the bare earth, wrapped in a blanket. There was also a single wooden chair and table, and that was all. The walls of the room did not extend all the way to the ceiling, and so the little family were daily exposed to sounds and events from neighbouring rooms that were, frankly, awful.

Rosemary's mother had reached grade one with her education, and so could only manage to get a job in a pub as a waitress. Here she worked hard for many years, doing her diligent best to raise her four children and nieces on next to nothing. Yet somehow, she also managed to pay Rosemary's school fees, to keep her in primary school.

When Rosemary was nine, news came that her father had died.

Her mother, bitter from years of rejection and struggle, refused to let any of the children go to the funeral. She wanted nothing to do with her husband and his family.

Rosemary's mother then somehow managed to get Rosemary into secondary school, where her outstanding ability at maths was soon evident. With the help of a scholarship, Rosemary had finished secondary school, a teaching certificate, and qualified for university. She had just done her first year in double-maths at Kenyatta University when tragedy struck again: her mother died.

That had left Rosemary, at only 21, as the head of the vulnerable little family; her siblings were then 19, 15 and 12. There were few relatives to help out, since her mother had been the first-born, and the rest of the family had looked up to her mother. As the title of Rosemary's own book tells it, Against all Odds, if she had not been strong in her Christian faith, she would have been destroyed.

So when, after all that struggle, Rosemary's grandmother heard that Rosemary wanted to marry someone from the small Mbeere tribe, she was incredulous. The Mbeere were considered to be backward. As her grandmother scornfully put it: "Mbeere are not good for anything! We used to cut off their ears!"

Sadly, this was literally true. Rosemary's grandmother had been in the Mau Mau movement that fought for Kenya's independence from the British. The British white settlers had wanted the Kikuyu lands (known as the White Highlands), as they were fertile. Conversely, the whites had not wanted the remote dry low-lands of the Mbeere tribe. So, when the Kikuyu, and also the neighbouring Embu tribe, demanded that the Mbeere come and help them attack the white man, the Mbeere were not very interested.

To be fair to the Mbeere, the wider reasons for the struggle were not explained to them. They simply reasoned that, as no one was bothering them, why should they risk their lives to start fighting the whites? But when the Kikuyu had insisted, unfortunately the Mbeere had resisted both them and the Embu (their cousins and perennial historical enemies) by attacking both tribes ferociously with bows and arrows (which they were famous for) as opposed to going for the white man!

So, then the Kikuyu had hated the Mbeere. When they captured a Mbeere, they would often cut off their ears with their pangas, as a mark of revenge , saying "these are the ones that refused to join us in fighting the white man". They despised the Mbeere for refusing to join the struggle, and of course the Mbeere deeply resented the Kikuyu for the humiliation of having their ears cut off!

This was the reason why Rosemary's grandmother and few aunts and uncles were not impressed with her wanting to marry a Mbeere. Indeed, during those early days with her family, every time I met her grandmother, she would cry aloud comically and clap her hands with a laugh: "Here is one of those Mbeere whose ears we cut off! But you still have your ears!" And she would roar with laughter. As she was by then more than 80, I could only respond by smiling sheepishly back at her.

Negotiating the bride price

Having to negotiate our wedding on top of such tribal prejudices, it was no wonder that we struggled. Indeed, for the first few months of our engagement, Rosemary and I did not make much progress.

Patiently, I just kept bringing Rosemary to visit my family, until over time they accepted the idea of our marriage. Rosemary's character and prudence slowly won her the respect of my dad, mum and siblings. Gradually, that respect would become real affection.

As for me, I was invited to meet not just the grandmother, but also the few uncles and aunts, and was of course 'looked over'.

When both families had finally agreed that their son and daughter could marry, the formal day for negotiating the wedding was set.

This day, known as the Uthoni day, is a very serious make-or-break day, when the families meet to negotiate the bride-price (also known as dowry).

My parents and relatives – uncles, aunties and close friends (about fifteen to twenty) arrived at Rosemary's grandmother's compound in Mwiki, Kasarani. We were welcomed to the compound and shown places to sit. Food was served; a goat had been slaughtered for the ceremony.

Then the bargaining began. The various uncles and aunts did the talking. Rosemary was up for sale; and she wasn't even allowed to be in the room. I was in the room, but not allowed to speak. This was older folk stuff and we were to rely on their bargaining power and hopefully they would agree on me 'buying this girl'. The term for marriage in both our tribes' languages (Mbeere & Kikuyu) is 'kugura' – i.e. buying! That is our Kenyan Mbeere and Kikuyu culture!

Rosemary's family was certainly true to their Kikuyu reputation for being good business people; they were very demanding over the bride-price.

Rosemary was first-born, that put her price up.

She had just graduated from University, that put her price even higher.

Each uncle and aunt and even the granny claimed they had invested in her after her mother had died. That put her price much higher again.

In fact, they used everything they could think of to raise the price. They finally put her on offer to us for 120 goats. It was an enormous price, and well in keeping with Kikuyu culture, to charge the highest price for a valued Kikuyu woman.

My uncle, leading my family's onslaught in return, pointed out that I was equally highly educated, and also the first-born.

But Rosemary's family was a brick wall: the price was 120 goats, some blankets and lessos (wrappers women tie around the waist), boots and coats. Each goat was at that time about Ksh 2000 (USD20). Today it would be equivalent to Ksh 6000 (USD60). Back then, the total came to about Ksh 240,000 (USD2400). Today, that would be the equivalent of Ksh 720,000 (USD7,200).

How on earth would I ever raise such an amount?! Even with my wider family support and friends, how were we to ever raise so much money? We were not at all sure!

To break the deadlock, one of my wiser relatives suggested a time out! 'Uthoni' negotiations can be very delicate. So, we quietly and sheepishly walked out, leaving our hosts seated, with a feeling of having won the first round.

Finding 120 goats

Once outside, it was time to come up with a fundraising strategy. I produced the Ksh 5000 (USD 50) that I had managed to save towards the bride-price. It represented an entire month's salary.

My dad, too, had brought some money: Ksh 7,000 (USD 70). Again, this was quite an amount for him, but still way too little to 'buy this girl'! My father told us some jokes to lighten the tension, but I knew he was thinking to himself: "I warned Stephen about these Kikuyu; now we are trapped!"

Many of my relatives there that day were obviously thinking the same thing; this was their first marriage 'out' from the Mbeere tribe, and they were appalled at the price set by Rosemary's family.

Inwardly, I was praying that they would not give up on me and my beloved girl–in-the-red-coat!

My dad must have seen my tense face, and guessed what was going on in my heart, for he then briskly rallied all our relatives. Just how much could all of us together raise? Relatives and friends dug around in their pockets and finally came up with an additional about

Ksh 3000 (USD 30), bringing it all to a total of Ksh 15,000 (USD 150). So, we all proceeded back into the house, hoping that this big amount might elicit some sort of positive reception.

My Uncle Stephen, being our chief negotiator, took up the bargaining again. He reminded everyone of the traditional etiquette that paying the bride-price never ends, and that marriage was a life-long relationship between both families. He then explained that we had raised Ksh 15,000 for immediate down-payment, and that we would keep the payments going on, long after the marriage. And so the negotiations went on.

(Just to explain this: it is the tradition, in both Mbeere and Kikuyu cultures, that you never finish paying the whole bride price. It was seen as a cultural safeguard for the woman, that you never own her. That way you are less likely to mistreat her or beat her up. Thus, by being forever indebted to the bride's family, the proper balance between the families is maintained. That was our culture at its best. To have paid all 120 goats at once for Rosemary would have been as if I had said to her uncles that their niece was so cheap that she could be bought outright.)

While both Rosemary and I wanted to honour our families, and do it properly – i.e., follow the customs, nevertheless that day I felt very discouraged. The amount that they were demanding for Rosemary was simply beyond us. After all the weeks of tension with my family, I suddenly felt almost like giving up. It was all too much of an uphill struggle for me, I was so discouraged. As we left her family, after a hard day's bargaining for my beloved Rosemary, I sent up a sad, dejected prayer to God.

The Lord encouraged me with some understanding that came as an impression into my heart. "Well, you love her, so pay the bride price. I loved the Church and paid the price for My bride. If you seriously love her, go for her and don't give up." And then a line of Scripture came into my mind that warmed me up and lifted my discouragement: "Husbands love your wives, as Christ loved the Church and gave Himself up for her." (Ephesians 5:28) Remembering what Jesus had paid for me gave me new resolve. He paid for me with His blood. In my case it was only money, and to me she was worth much more than 120 goats!

So in the end, somehow, eight goats (Ksh 16,000 or USD160) were bought and handed over as 'down payment'. Later, we were able to give another Ksh 30,000 (USD 300) which was 15 more goats, and the bride-price journey was slowly underway.

Then, laboriously, all the arrangements for our wedding were put into place.

Finally, on 1st April 1995, we held a big church wedding at the Living Word Church in Pangani, a suburb of Nairobi. Our Bishop, Silas Peter Kiio, presided over the ceremony.

And I mean BIG!

Guests were pouring in from both extended families, from my parents' church, from Rosemary's church, from my Daystar University years, from Rosemary's school and her university years, and so on. A delegation even came down from my village! There were several hundred people there that day. The women prepared an awesome wedding feast for us all.

We honeymooned down the coast at Malindi, several hundred kilometres to the south. My Team Leader, Gershon, and the AE Team had bought our bus ticket to Malindi. This was such a blessing to me and Rosemary.

When we got to Malindi, I discovered that Rosemary had never eaten a pizza. So we started our married life with a pizza at the hotel, celebrating and thanking God that He had given us each other. Finally, we had made it: we were married!

Back home after the honeymoon, we discovered that the wedding celebrations were still going on. By now the people in my home village of Kavengero in Kanyuambora (Mbeere) who had not been able to get down to Nairobi were demanding that we go up to them. It was only a week after our wedding, so they wanted us to stage the wedding ceremony all over again.

So, we went to Kavengero in Kanyuambora. We were glad to do so. It was a way for me to honour my dad and mum, by showing the village that their son was not 'lost in the city', but still wanted to be a valued part of their upcountry home village community.

Rosemary put her wedding dress back on, and I put on my wedding suit. We repeated our vows again, in front of most of the village. Once again, a huge feast followed the ceremony, held at the Kavengero primary school. The village blessed us with marriage presents of hand-woven baskets, chickens and even some cash!

Finally, having gone through two weddings and two feasts in a space of two weeks, we returned to Nairobi, a tired and yet happy young couple, eager to begin our married life together.

'It was just the amount we needed!'

10
Learning to Trust God for Everything

Many are the woes of the wicked, but the Lord's unfailing love surrounds the one who trusts in him. - Psalm 32:10

The early days of our marriage were spent in the smallest home you could ever imagine. We had rented a two-room mud house, plastered with cement on the outside, on Wanyee Road, Dagorretti in Nairobi. There was a bedroom which was only just a few inches bigger than our bed, a sitting room with a couple of chairs and a table, and then a tiny walk-in kitchen with a shelf and a sink. When we wanted to cook local foods such as maize and beans, we had to build a fire outside. Any guests or relatives had to sleep on a mat and blanket in the tiny sitting room.

Even so, we struggled to pay the bills at times. However, we were so happy to have a place of our own to call home! We were well aware that there were many who lived in much more humble dwellings than ours, and many who began their married lives in far more difficult circumstances.

Life was undeniably tough, but God was good, and He used the most unlikely of people to encourage me. Our neighbourhood was swampy and prone to flooding, and there were many deep, rubbish-strewn puddles. One day as I was dashing for the bus to go to work, I was grumbling to myself about all the mud that was splashing onto my trousers. But as I ran, I encountered one of our neighbours, an old lady who lived alone in a tin hut that was even smaller than our mud house.

That hut was actually on the edge of what we called the 'Congo slums' because of all the Congolese refugees who lived in that vicinity. However, most of the days as I passed her, I would hear this lady cheerfully singing praises to the Lord as she washed her dishes or clothes outside. I did not need to be told she was a Christian! For somehow, rather than living in misery due to her surroundings – the great puddles of filthy water, no running water, and a shared pit latrine outside – she was always joyful.

That particular morning, she was washing her few dishes outside in her bucket and stacking them carefully on the ground, because she did not even have a board on which to dry them. Yet her song, to my memory, went something like: "Lord I lift your name on high. I love to sing your praises. I am so glad you are in my life. You came from heaven to earth to show the way…"

As I passed by her, trying to avoid the puddles, I was deeply touched by her infectious cheerfulness. It was in such stark contrast to my own impatience and depression with all the filth and the wet. Such things did not seem to affect her one bit: she was singing cheerfully, and smiling to herself (or to the Lord) as I went by.

So then, I felt ashamed. I knew that the Lord was saying to me: "The joy of the Lord should prevail over your circumstances." That lady, who was living in such obvious poverty, taught me a valuable lesson! She never knew how much she had rebuked and yet encouraged and uplifted me that day, and often I have recalled her courage and faith, and shared her story.

Beyond boundaries

But our living near the 'Congo' slums, amidst puddles and mud, was paradise compared to what awaited me in July 1995. For only three months after our marriage, I left Nairobi in order to join in a major AE mission to Kigali. Rwanda was in ruins after the terrible genocide of 1994, and all of AE teams from across Africa had been summoned to Kigali. We had been asked to encourage the churches, and to minister to the broken people of Rwanda.

By then I had been Missions Director for AE Kenya for nearly two years. I had seen some very rough things on my various travels around the country, and they had opened my eyes as to the abyss of spiritual need that there was across East Africa. I had also begun to see God fulfilling His promise to me: that I would be sent to preach across boundaries in many countries, in a way beyond anything I had imagined was possible. I had kept coming back to those words He had given me in Isiolo: From the reached to the unreached. From the possible to the impossible.

And now, in Rwanda, I was up against horror that I had never dreamed of in my worst nightmares. This was a case of helping both 'the reached' and 'the unreached' as they tried to come to terms with 'the impossible'.

For in 1994, more than 800,000 Rwandans had been slaughtered during a 100-day period between the months of April and June. This was genocide beyond imagination, and beyond the experience of anyone living in Africa.

Tragically, three of our seven AE staff members had also been killed. They included Israel Havugimana, our then AE Rwanda Team Leader. We mourned news of his death with heavy hearts. Israel, although a Hutu, and therefore of the dominant tribe, had been known to speak out in defence of the Tutsi, even on radio! He had openly called for reconciliation with them. Little wonder, then, that when the genocide had begun, he was among the first to be killed. But not just him – the killers had slaughtered his wife and children as well, with the exception of his tiniest little daughter, whom they had left for dead in the bloody mess of the home.

Of course, Israel's family was just one of hundreds of thousands of families who had lost loved ones. My current colleague and AE International Missions Director, Emmanuel Kwizera, had lost about 100 of his wider family members. Rwanda was in deep shock and grief, but thankfully, all kinds of help was pouring in from around the world. In July 1995 all our AE teams converged on Kigali, wanting to do our bit in showing solidarity and in aiding this small nation that was so deeply traumatised. We were led by Michael Cassidy, our founder and International Team Leader, who had also invited along Archbishop Desmond Tutu, Nobel Peace Prize winner and a long-time friend of his from South Africa.

Horror in Rwanda

Our objective was simple: to bring God's comfort and love to this grief-stricken country, and to minister the message of His peace and reconciliation. We were also keen to encourage our Rwandan team. Since Israel's murder, we had appointed a new leader, Antoine Rutayasire, who had previously been on the AE Rwandan board. Antoine, while from a different tribe with Israel, had been one of Israel's prayer partners. The week preceding his killing they had spent time together in prayer and Bible study that Israel hosted in his house. They prayed for hours for their nation, and were planning a nation-wide prayer meeting. Now, following the slaughter, Antoine had his work cut out for him, for members of the AE Rwandan team were seriously hurting, having lost not just Israel, but other colleagues as well, and many of their relatives.

Going to Rwanda in July 1995, even nearly a year after the genocide, was still very dangerous. People were still being killed in Rwanda on a regular basis – as grieving relatives of the dead took their revenge when and where they could. The rule of law was very fragile. In fact, it was a fearful country to visit, and so Rosemary and I prayed fervently for the protection of the team.

Our team landed at Kigali Airport, and we made our way carefully into the city. The beginnings of most missions are cheerful, noisy, optimistic affairs. But, not this one. We gathered at the small AE Rwandan offices in a very sombre frame of mind. We would be reaching out to people whose family members had been hacked into pieces in front of their eyes, whose hearts had been broken, and who were, even now, barely able to function on a daily basis.

As we drove around the city, I was in shock. I had never seen anything like this and prayed that neither I nor anyone would live to see this again. The number of dead were beyond counting. We visited site after site, stacked high with human skulls. Many of the skulls still had pieces of metal imbedded in them, such as machetes. (A YouTube footage of our visit is available: https://www.youtube.com/watch?v=65L9jtejbyw.) There is one poignant moment in that footage where Archbishop Desmond Tutu began to weep in public, just broken by the sights we were encountering. Many of us from AE were in tears as well.

What could we possibly say that would bring any comfort to the survivors of such an outrage? We knew it was completely beyond us. But we were not there on our own, we had come in the name of Jesus Christ. So, with much prayer and humility, we went into the churches of Kigali and into the prisons, seeking only to bring them a message of divine hope and encouragement.

In the churches and in the prisons the survivors talked to us. The horror of what they told us broke us all down. We wept with them, and that weeping became a part of each meeting. It was the only possible response to stories that were beyond belief: of how some church ministers, in a frenzy of tribalistic hatred, had betrayed members of their own congregations who had come to them for refuge – and while pretending to hide them, had called in the killers, who slaughtered them as sheep without a shepherd. We were told of husbands and wives in mixed marriages who had betrayed their own spouses to the militia, and then stood by and watched them being slaughtered. What madness was this?! We found it unbelievable.

Yet in the midst of such unutterable darkness, some people had stood out like shining stars. In one church, the militia had come and ordered the whole congregation to stand in one part of the building. The militia had then ordered that all the people who were not Tutsi should get out of the way, so that the Tutsi could be killed. But, it did not happen! The entire congregation stood still. They said that they all belonged to one family, God's family.

So – the militia had killed them all: Tutsi and Hutu together. What an incredible witness that God's love goes beyond tribal lines. It was not forgotten, either, for in later years some of the militia who had taken part that day were themselves converted, and they spoke of the great effect that the congregation had had on them in sticking together.

Only the Cross

So many stories from that mission remain deeply entrenched in my memory. One account was from a young sister in Christ who accompanied us to the various sites. She shared with us how in the Rwandan genocide of 1959 all her mother's family members were killed, with her mother alone surviving. Then she shared with us how, in this 1994 genocide, all her relatives, brothers and sisters, had been wiped out, and now she alone remained. She was in deep distress and lived in the greatest fear that in the future, history would likely repeat itself a third time.

Such was the kind of traumatised humanity that we encountered. What could we possibly say to someone like that? What answers could we give to the many who were bitter and seeking for revenge?

While not being simplistic, the only solution we knew was to point them gently up to the Cross – to the one that cried out "Lord forgive them, for they do not know what they are doing."

Throughout the mission, while we listened and gave all the encouragement we could, we knew that such wounds would take years to heal, and that at the end, the Cross would have to become their ultimate place of solace. From time to time in our meetings, we invited those who were willing to come to the front to pin their pain onto the cross hanging at the front. It was a way for them to visually seek relief from the horrors they had witnessed. Some had seen many die right in front of their eyes, some had been raped many times. Whatever it was, we saw that the tearful un-burdening of their hearts on Jesus' cross became the start of real healing. Many of them, after that mission, went on themselves to become ministers of healing and reconciliation. Antoine's book Faith Under Fire captures some of these accounts.

Desmond Tutu

At a time such as this, to have joint-leaders such as Michael Cassidy and Bishop Desmond Tutu was a godsend. They led the bigger, more high-profile meetings, and being black and white South Africans working together, despite the painful decades of apartheid in South Africa, was such a strong witness to the city. Reconciliation and unity was possible, here was the proof! And their partnership and sharing from South Africa's experience meant that some major national doors were opened to us, including a Top Leadership dinner with the incoming Prime Minister Paul Kagame, who had led the liberation. (He later became President)

Desmond Tutu's message to the church in Rwanda, as they struggled to find an answer to 'where was God in all this?' was the poignant message from chapter three of the book of Daniel, the story of Shadrach, Meshach and Abednego. They had been thrown into the merciless fiery flames of the furnace, and yet, the Lord was with them IN the flames. As Nebuchadnezzar had said: "we put three men into the furnace, and yet I see a fourth – and he looks like the Son of God." Yes, even in those worst, grievous moments, He, Emmanuel, God, is right there with us!

After such an emotional and draining mission as that to Rwanda, I was glad to return to Nairobi, Rosemary and our little mud house. The large puddles were still there, but now I wondered why a bit of mud and water had ever troubled me, after what I had just seen.

Egypt

Another highlight of my years as Missions Director at AE Kenya took place in 1996, when our AE Kenya team was invited by various churches in Egypt to hold a mission with them.

Egypt, in spite of its long Christian heritage, with famous 'church fathers' such as Tertullian (of Alexandria), is a very Islamic country, and so it would be a challenging place for Christian evangelism. Our team flew together to Cairo, where I was assigned to Tanta, a city in the Delta region towards Alexandria.

I had to go alone there to preach, instead of taking a companion, as was usual. The places wanting ministry were so many that we could not follow our usual pattern of going two by two. Had I known what lay ahead, without any AE support around me, I would have been very daunted. Sometimes, it is good not to know what is coming next! However, the Egyptian Christians wanted us to visit as many centres as we could, and so we were spread out very thin on the ground.

On first arrival in Tanta, I had some very uncomfortable moments, based on just basic cultural differences. For instance, I wore a bright red African outfit that was much admired in Kenya; here, to my dismay, it caused great hilarity. I discovered that in the Arab world, red is a colour only women wear!

As if finding out that I was dressed like a woman was not embarrassing enough, my male Egyptian host then firmly took my hand to lead me through the streets. This was apparently the local custom, and showed the guest great honour, but I felt very discomfited. I did not want to wander about city streets holding hands with a man whom I had just met, even if he was a Christian, and nor did I want people to burst into giggles when they saw what I was wearing. All in all, I was glad to get back to the hotel!

Then there were cultural problems with some of my preaching. One day I was preaching about Jesus riding the humble little donkey into Jerusalem, and I added that we all need to "be donkeys for Jesus," or in other words, to carry and bring Jesus into people's lives and into our various day-to-day chores.

At that point my host minister who was also my translator, who spoke both English and Arabic smiled in a manner that suggested something wasn't totally okay. He later explained that he had had to change what I had said. Apparently in Egypt a donkey is seen as stupid and slow, just an animal kept for its usefulness, an animal sadly used and misused and abused. The correlation would have been speaking to a western audience and telling them – be a chicken for Jesus, or in an African context, be a cow for Jesus!

Encountering a demon

But then something happened which cut across all cultural boundaries. The Christians in Tanta had been reaching out to various Muslim families, and several of the Muslims had responded by saying that they were struggling with relatives back at home whom they feared were demon-possessed. They had begged us to pray for them. I had encountered some witchcraft and demon-possession in Kenya, of course, but up until then (1996) I had never tackled it on my own.

That all changed one evening at the end of our service, when we invited people forward for prayer. A hefty Muslim man and a younger man came forward, leading a young Muslim woman dressed in a hijab. The hefty man, with his Islamic cap still on, explained that he was her father, and that this was her brother. He said they needed help, because his daughter had a demon. She was 22 years old and had been suffering since she was 14. She had not been able to go to school for seven years, because of her violence. If she even heard someone reading the Quran, the demon would react, and she would become hysterical. The family was therefore desperately seeking help for her.

At first, I was sceptical: perhaps they had really come here to cause trouble? We had been warned back in Cairo that sometimes Muslims did this in Christian services. The authorities had already stationed two policemen at the door of our church, to stop any Muslims who wanted to come in and convert to Christianity. But we knew the policemen were also there to spy on us Christians; as to whether or not we were speaking against Islam. So, I was surprised that the man and his son and daughter had even made it past the police.

But the father and brother kept insisting that she had a demon, though she didn't look like she did. She was well-dressed and calm and looked about the church meeting with interest.

However, as soon as I began to pray for her, she grew agitated. She began fretting and moaning. Then she let out a terrible shriek. The hairs on the back of my neck stood up! She followed this by scream after scream, as I and some leaders in the church continued to pray for her. Then she reached out to scratch and kick me, but her father and brother held on to her grimly. They had obviously expected this!

Well, we prayed, and we prayed, but got nowhere. Suddenly, to my astonishment, some of the church leaders began to actually slap the young woman. Their motive seemed to be partly to vent their frustration, and partly to scare the demon out.

Of course, it did not work. But sadly, there are many Christians, even today, who follow such unbiblical practices. Instead, of course, their slapping only terrified the poor woman more. She had enough problems with the demon that was afflicting her!

So, I continued to pray and pray over that young woman, until I was literally sweating over her. But, still nothing happened. So finally, being the guest and therefore in charge, I called a halt to the proceedings. We were all totally exhausted. I moved on and began praying for other people's needs.

The following day we held another service, and again, at the end of my message many people came forward for prayer. So many of them were ill, and wanting healing, that I almost wondered if the Egyptian Christians had put out the word that I was some sort of a miracle worker! By the time I got to the end of ministering to the people, I and all those who were assisting me were well exhausted and fully drenched in sweat, as we had been ministering in the Egyptian heat, devoid of any cooling system. But just as I thought we were done, the Muslim woman who had exhausted us the previous night was brought forward again, seeking prayer.

I felt a wave of some dismay sweep over me, and also great surprise. After my total failure with her the evening before, I had expected her family to give up on us praying for her. But, no, here they were back again, still hoping we could help her.

Take off the hijab

As I finally reached her and greeted her, I decided what I would do. I would lay hands on her, to give her some psychological reassurance that I had prayed for her, and then release her quickly, and move on. I felt simply too tired to get into the same sort of drama as the night before. I was facing an impossible task – and one whose failure to conquer the night before was still too fresh. Inwardly, I also hoped that my simple laying-on of hands would not stir up the evil spirit, and I was right – the girl remained quiet. But now something stirred within me. I sensed God putting the thought into my mind: "if she removes her hijab, she will be healed."

My mind began to race: how could I possibly ask such a thing? Muslim women never take off their hijab in front of men who are not in their family. No, I decided: this can't be advice from the Lord. So, I said nothing, and following my one minute or so of prayer, the lady and family went away again. Back at my accommodation that night, I felt very uncomfortable – I wondered if I had not disobeyed the Lord's prompting. If so, I had let both Him and that poor lady down. But the good Lord, who knows our weaknesses and our measure of faith, is forgiving and often gives us more chances.

For the following morning, they were back yet again! Again, we called on God, and again we demanded that the demon leave. As if following one of the stories from the Bible, the demon verbally refused. And the girl, although so tiny, became supernaturally strong. Her father and brother were thrown off her, as she flew at us like a wildcat, hissing like a snake. A number of men grabbed her just in time, but even so, they could barely restrain her.

As I looked into her tormented, furious face, filled with such hatred and evil and yet desperation, I could feel nothing but compassion on one who was so tortured. And so, for the next hour or so, we prayed and shouted at that demon to leave.

I finally stood back, in exhaustion and was about to give up. Then the Lord brought to my memory the impression of the previous day: "She needs to take her hijab off, and she will be delivered."

As this thought grew stronger in my mind, I told everyone to stop the racket we had all been making, and softly, with hesitation, I repeated what the Lord had said: "The Lord is leading me to say to you that if you take off the hijab you will be delivered."

The father and brother were shocked at my suggestion, and looked at me wide-eyed as if to say: "do you know what you are asking of us?" My hosts were equally taken by surprise. But I had nothing else to say. We had tried everything else, and they could take or leave my suggestion. I had simply said what was in my mind, and I fervently hoped that it would work, or I would be totally put to shame!

The father and son regained their composure and exchanged looks. I could see that they were willing to try it. But alas, the poor girl, though exhausted from all the drama, absolutely and openly refused. Her father and brother took her to one side and began pleading with her, to try what this stranger was saying, to "remove the hijab and you will be healed."

I was later to learn that for a Muslim woman to remove her hijab in public is like being naked. The hijab to them is the outward sign of their inward virtue. In the presence of non-immediate close male relatives, the hijab is part of Islamic modesty. And so she firmly said no!

But, upon reflecting later, I came to see that the reason that the hijab was such a barrier to her healing was precisely because it represented her understanding of faith and virtue in relation to God. Her righteousness was based on her own self-sanctity, as taught by Islam. What, in spiritual terms, we were asking her to do instead was to stop believing in her good works as means of being righteous before God, and instead to come to Jesus, just as she was. That was why the Lord had put it in my mind that she needed to take off her hijab.

After many minutes of whispered pleading, the father and brother finally prevailed on the girl to take off her hijab. She was wearing a long black one, which went from her head all the way down to her waist.

Released and at peace

Reluctantly she stood and slowly removed the top part of her hijab. Energised by her cooperation, we again engaged in earnest prayer. As I said "in the name of Jesus come out", she screamed and was flung again to the floor. We demanded that the demon leave her, in Jesus' name. And, within a matter of about two minutes, she was free! We could all feel a great evil depart from her body. It was followed by peace. The speed and the ease of her release and the evident victory and peace, compared to the commotion we had all been having to make left me feeling frustrated. We had wasted so much time and energy!

The girl now lay limply on the floor, her features relaxing from hatred and frenzy into those of a vulnerable, exhausted young woman. She lay quite still, and then opened her eyes, and looked around. She saw her father. Tentatively, she smiled up at him. And he began to weep, as he reached down to her. "This is my daughter," he cried, "she has come back to me again." There was no more torment. The father and son's excitement was so evident. The change, peace, calmness and serenity depicted by their daughter was so obvious!

The father then looked at me and to my surprise said, "How much do I owe you?"

To his astonishment, of course we refused all money. Instead, we told him about the verse in Matthew 10:8: 'freely you have received; freely give'. We told him that the greatest gift of all that he could have was God's Son.

We explained to them again that it was Jesus who had healed the girl, not us. It was through Jesus that they could experience the greatest miracle of all, having their sins forgiven. And it was through Jesus that they could actually have a personal relationship with God! When they heard that, the father, the brother and the girl were converted there and then – they all wanted this Jesus. Fortunately, the police at the church door did not seem to notice.

Over a much-needed break, we were to learn that we had been their last hope. For nearly eight years they had spent large amounts of money on doctor after doctor, and on traditional medicine men/women including witch-doctors, with no results. They had gone to various mosques, begging the imams for help, but with no results. Finally, one imam just the previous week (before our mission and encounter) had admitted that the mosque had nothing else to offer. But as they prepared to leave him, he must have been moved by their obvious desperation. For suddenly, the imam had blurted out: "Go and seek help from the church. Their Jesus as written in the Injili (Gospels) used to heal sick people and free those oppressed by demons. Go to the Christians." And so, they had come to us.

The father, the brother and the sister then went home, but they were back again for the evening service. The church members greeted the family with real joy and love, as word had got around about the girl's healing.

But the father still had another surprise for us. He had hauled along a large sophisticated-looking pouch, and now showed me the contents: it was full of witchcraft charms and other paraphernalia which they had been given over time by various would-be healers. "I don't want these," he told me. "They are useless. What do I do with them?"

That was easy! I spoke to the church leaders, and right there inside the church we put the charms into a metal container and poured paraffin on them and set them ablaze. This was followed by jubilation, as we all sang loudly, and danced, celebrating and giving God praise for the freedom and victory accorded to the girl.

We were so excited and joyful that we all but forgot the watchful eyes of the policemen who were at the church entrance. But as they had followed our proceedings over several days, they appeared equally happy that the girl had been set free.

That night I fell into bed both utterly exhausted and elated at the same time - what an experience! This was my first time on a mission in Islamic North Africa, far from home, and then to experience firsthand a case of demonic deliverance.

That mission was a turning point for me. Another great lesson had been learned: it was important to prayerfully discern the spiritual reality of a situation, and then to deal with that, rather than simply broadside a problem with enthusiastic, but indiscriminate, prayer.

And I knew now that in such situations I could ask God to guide me in what to pray, and what to do. I had also learnt the importance of listening for the Holy Spirit's promptings. His guidance might come at the most unexpected moment, and I needed to heed His leading with courage. Heeding could save me both time and the pain of trying to do things that were simply never going to work. The key to doing the impossible was to listen to His Spirit and leading!

Serving the Lord together

It was wonderful to be back in Nairobi again, both with Rosemary at home, and also with the supportive team at our office. But it reminded me that there was a strain growing in our marriage which I was not sure how to handle. How were we ever going to combine our ministries because Rosemary also had a passion for preaching and evangelism? During our courtship one of the things we had discussed and anticipated was the pleasure of doing ministry together. After all, our first encounters and even my proposal of "will you marry me" were all in the context of missions!

I had been appointed Mission Director at AE Kenya in late 1994, and we had married the following April. Rosemary would have loved to have joined me on the AE team at that point, but, unlike Campus Crusade, AE did not run on the model of having husbands and wives working together in ministry. So when we were first married, Rosemary had taken a volunteer post at Rebuilders for Christ. It was a Christian ministry in Nairobi, led by Peterson Rukenya, a good friend and contemporary of ours.

But since Peterson was not full-time with Rebuilders at that point, Rosemary often found herself all alone at the Rebuilders office as well. She therefore was left to create work for herself, and then do it alone. Her other team members mostly did only weekend ministry to schools and churches.

So I was in mission and evangelism, and Rosemary was on the

fringes. When AE did big missions, and we needed all the people we could get, Rosemary was desperately keen to come along and help. That would have been fine with AE, but most of the time, there was simply no money to pay for her ticket. Once I managed to afford to take her along on a mission at Meru, where she preached and led the singing and really threw herself into it. We had had a wonderful mission together!

It was only once a year, when I was gone for weeks at a time on a really large city-wide mission, that finance was found for her to come along. But the rest of the time, month after month, Rosemary was left out of AE work.

A few months after my trip to Egypt, in early 1997, Rosemary and I finally reached a crisis over the problem. It became a pivotal point in my learning of the need to rely on God first, and then AE, for our ministry needs.

I was busy setting up a mission in Nakuru, one of Kenya's towns. I was to go up for the weekend, meet with the ministers to plan the mission, and then preach in some Nakuru churches before returning. Rosemary watched my preparations with deepening gloom. Finally, she said: "It seems you are the only one who will have the fun of going, because AE will not pay for both of us to go." She looked so unhappy.

I felt the familiar wave of frustration sweep over me. The memories of our talks and prayers before marriage of how we would serve the Lord together were haunting me. But the office had given me only 500 Kenyan shillings (about five dollars) fare for the whole trip. Rosemary felt that AE had not been considerate, in not giving enough for both of us to go. We discussed it at length, and that afternoon I suddenly felt led to say that I felt we should go together to Nakuru.

So then, all that I needed to do was to pray in the extra money! "After all," I said to myself, "just because AE cannot supply, that is not the end of the matter. God is bigger than AE."

We lived near a church, and I went down there that evening and prayed for about two hours, until suddenly I felt an assurance that God was going to supply the means for Rosemary to come along. Upon getting back to the house, I told Rosemary that I had the assurance that we should go together. I then encouraged her to sleep, so as to be ready for the journey, and to trust my feelings over it.

But I did not convince her! She knew the reality of the situation: there was still 500 Ksh between her and that trip, and we both knew we did not have that much money. If we had it – we would gladly have been all set to go.

Nevertheless, early the following morning I got ready and encouraged her to do the same. She was still grumpy with AE, but she finally got ready too, and we were ready to go. As was our common practice, we stood at the door and joined hands to pray and ask God for a safe journey. As we were just about to pray, we heard a knock at the door. We paused in astonishment – who was visiting us this early in the morning? It was only 7am!

The exact amount

It turned out to be a neighbour from down the way. She said she had a letter for us that someone had left with her the previous day when we were not at home. She thought she had better deliver it this morning. So, we thanked her, she went home, and we set off for the bus stop. On the way I casually opened the letter - and inside was 500 shillings (USD 5). Just the amount – equivalent to what I had received from the office – the exact amount that we needed!

What a huge encouragement to our faith! God is bigger than us, and His ways of provision will not be limited. It was an important lesson to remember; that even when you are within the structure of an organisation, or when you have the security of family and friends and church all round you, still, ultimately, your provision always comes from God. The Psalmist sums this upward look attitude so well "I lift up my eyes unto the hills, where does my help come from. My help comes from the Lord the maker of heaven and earth." (Psalm 121)

That 500 Ksh gift in an envelope was such an inspiration. We knew then that we did not have to look just to AE for resources. For me, it was the follow-on to the earlier lesson – "Don't just look to your dad and mum, because where I will send you, you will be on your own." It also underscored what the Lord had quickened into my heart during my hide-away time in Isiolo: "the labourer deserves his dues" (Matthew 10:10). As well as food, rent, and clothing, it seemed that that verse also covered transport for wives!

'The nurses were firm: men were NOT allowed to be at the baby's birth!'

11
Further Studies and Parenthood

Your wife will be like a fruitful vine within your house; your children will be like olive shoots around your table. Yes, this will be the blessing for the man who fears the Lord. - Psalm 128:3,4

By the late summer of 1996 it was time to move out of our tiny home on Wanyee Road.

Rosemary had long felt called to do full-time Christian ministry of some sort, but she was not as prepared for it as she wanted to be. Her first degree had been in double maths in Kenyatta University's faculty of Education. This of course was a specialised subject, with nothing to do with theology! So, she had decided to pursue a Master's degree in Christian Education, which would also make good use of her very first qualification as a teacher.

Some friends had told us about NEGST, which had begun in 1983 as the Nairobi Evangelical Graduate School of Theology. It is presently a part of Africa International University (AIU). I took Rosemary for the interview, as she was visibly pregnant and I felt the need to support her. As we walked from the gate to the classes we were impressed by the atmosphere of the university. While not so big as some, the grounds and buildings were well kept and attractive.

Rosemary begins her Master's

I sat in as she answered various questions as to why she felt called to do a Masters in Christian Education. I kept wondering if I might ever have the chance to do a similar course. However, I guessed I was too busy doing missions, to even think of theological studies – once the cause of some tension between my dad and me.

It did not take long for us to learn that Rosemary had passed the interview. We were so excited that Rosemary was finally going to take a step towards what she felt was her calling – full-time Christian service. But we were surprised and excited even much more to learn that the university had student housing for married couples, and that she had qualified for a student apartment!

Our little family was now going to move from the mud and puddles of Wanyee Road to the comfort of Karen, an up-market suburb of Nairobi. Our new home was a small student flat in block Q4. Although we did not know it at the time, it would be our home for the next five years.

By the time we moved, Rosemary was heavily pregnant, so thankfully, our student flat was larger than our home on Wanyee Road had been. Now we were blessed with two bedrooms, solar heating and a kitchen with a stove and fridge - all provided by the school! The needs of the students had been well thought through and provided for. All that the student had to do, besides buying and cooking their food, was to study. We were very grateful for that flat and the accompanying arrangements – it was the nicest student accommodation we had ever seen.

Later, we discovered that the well-equipped student blocks had been made possible through the determination – and compassion – of African Christian leaders such as Byang Kato and, in later years,

Tokunboh Adeyemo. Both men had played a fundamental role in founding this university, with the generous support of mission agencies from around the world. Due to their hard work, students could study and live here at subsidised costs.

To pay the amount that was required of us, we organised a fundraising where we invited friends and relatives. My dad played a major role in helping us achieve this new milestone. He not only helped us organise, but he also invited some of his colleagues from Daystar. Some of his students including Bishop Katutu (of Destiny Church) came as Guests of Honour. We were therefore able to achieve our side of the bargain without so much of a challenge, courtesy of these friends.

Certainly, the student accommodation of block Q4 provided us with a 'good neighbourhood', for we were surrounded by a very supportive international community of students and members of staff. We thanked God for this wonderful, safe home in which we could begin raising our family.

As Christmas of 1996 approached, our baby was equally approaching. But let me retrace the journey to this point. When we married, Rosemary and I had made a commitment not to start our family quickly, so that we could spend the early months of our marriage getting to bond and to know each other. We had heard accounts of how the hormones of pregnancy can impact on the woman's temperament, and of how that in turn can impact on how the man and the wife relate.

Deciding to start our family

So, we delayed pregnancy until the first year was over. A few months into the second year, Rosemary's friends who had got married around the same time as we did began having babies. I recall one time we visited one of them, and Rosemary was holding their baby in her hands. The look in her eyes was telling, she wanted to hold her own child!

So, from that point on she began persuading me that it was time for us to have a child. We had hoped to wait for two years, but it was not going to be. I lost it! Rosemary wanted to hold her own child, and to breastfeed her own child. I have often used this story in preparing for missions and winning souls (i.e. people to Jesus) to press the point that we too should desire to see people being born into God's kingdom, passionately – without delay!

On 19th December Rosemary went into labour, and I rushed her to the Kikuyu Mission Hospital. We spent the day there, but the baby didn't seem to be in any hurry, and just wasn't being born.

The gynaecologist warned us that if our baby did not arrive the following day, then she would conduct a C-section. This was a great shock to both of us. We had really prayed that Rosemary would be able to have a normal birth.

For many more hours Rosemary really tried. We delayed that C-section as long as we dared, but it became inevitable. We were both deeply sad, for somehow, amongst our friends, it was seen as a lack of faith that a couple should not have their baby born naturally. Looking back now, I can see this sort of teaching was total nonsense, but at the time, it shadowed our perceptions.

But the gynaecologist reminded us that the main priority was the baby and mother's health! We must aim at saving both. Any delay could risk the health of either or both! Also, we were grateful that a C-section was even available, because in Kenya many women and babies have died in labour.

When the medical staff wheeled Rosemary off to the operating theatre, they left me disconsolate. My efforts to follow her had been firmly blocked: the nurse looked at me sternly and said: 'absolutely no!' In those days the delivery room was totally out of bounds for fathers. This was a woman's affair, according to established African custom. Those African nurses had no intention of letting me, the mere dad, into their domain!

Left alone, I fretted and paced. I walked around and around that maternity ward until I felt a bit like the Israelites prowling around the walls of Jericho. The nurses on the reception desk watched me with sympathy. I overheard one say to the other: "Poor boy. Obviously, it's his first-born."

What a relief it was when the nurse finally reappeared and called for me! I rushed after her and found Rosemary looking exhausted but very happy, holding our precious new son, Victor, in her arms. When a few years later our daughter Joy was born, I made sure to contact the gynaecologist well ahead of time, and get permission to be with Rosemary at the birth – in that same operating theatre! Thankfully, it was the same gynaecologist, and having shared with her my frustrations at the birth of our first born, she was understanding, and made arrangements for me to be there at Joy's birth.

Taking home the baby

On the day we were leaving hospital with Victor, dad and mum came to pick us up in their pick-up that we fondly called 'KUF'– due to its KUF number plate. It was a pick-up that had a front seat for driver and passenger, and then a wooden bench in the back. So Rosemary held the baby and sat at the front next to dad, and mum and I bounced along at the back.

Back home, the three of us settled into our new routine of life in student block Q4. Rosemary had only three weeks before she was due back in class, and she needed to get used to her new role. She loved being a mother and a student, but it wasn't easy balancing things, and so I gave her all the support I could. Thankfully, the school was much nearer to my office than the previous place we lived, given that my office was also in Karen.

Being a father was both exciting and daunting. First, I had to learn how to hold the baby. Then I had to learn how to help the baby to burp after breastfeeding. That was one of the more interesting skills of fatherhood for me. You rub the baby's back and hold them on your shoulder until they, so to say, 'vomit'- there is a technical word for this. Often it pours on your clothes, and from time to time you may go around smelling of baby's 'burp'! But that is the price of fatherhood.

Washing nappies was another lesson I had to learn, and fast! Rosemary had gone through a C-section and needed time to recover. We brought in a house-help to be with Rosemary while I was at work, but when I was home, I took the main share in caring for our precious baby. That included washing nappies, which was certainly one of the testing points of being a new father!

Disposable nappies were not common in those days, and we used the white cotton baby nappy. Soaking and scrubbing my way through dozens of soiled nappies gave me time to ponder a mystery: why on earth do the people who make baby nappies make them white? They must know that baby poo will make them brown!

As an African man, washing dirty clothes was not a usual thing to do, especially when you are at home, and even more so when you are married. But Rosemary and I were parents together, and she was recovering, so I washed the nappies and pinned them carefully out on the line to dry. People would often see me (or I would see them), and I wondered what they thought. Did they wonder why a man would do this job? Or did they wonder if I was man enough to do a good job and get those nappies really clean!

These were great fatherhood lessons that I learned. I still use them in mission settings, when I talk about caring for new believers.

The toughest part of parenthood for me was getting up in the night. Lots of times in the night! This Victor fellow loved being awake at night – and even today, well into his 20s, still does! In the early days I had to bring the baby to Rosemary to breastfeed. Slowly she got better, and then came the morning when I woke up and said: "Darling, the baby was good last night, he didn't wake up at all!"

Rosemary laughed. "You man! – he woke up several times!" Oh dear. I was still learning this fatherhood game!

Nairobi International School of Theology

A few months later, in 1997, I also returned to study. Having done my BA in Business Administration and not Theology, I was increasingly finding myself at a disadvantage in relating to the pastors in the bigger cities, where they tended to have had more education than pastors in rural areas. While I was fine with the strategy and organisation of missions, the pastors would often ask me what theological credentials I held. I could see that the fact that I had had no formal theological training stood somewhat against me, and that, while excited by my strategizing, they were vaguely disappointed that I didn't have theological credentials. Plus, when various theological debates arose, I could find myself on shaky ground. I therefore decided that I should also pursue my Master's, at the Nairobi International School of Theology, currently International Leadership University (ILU).

Getting leave to study and work only part-time at AE Kenya was not easy. There was no precedence. It took a lot of discussions within our team as to how we could possibly manage the workload if I was not full-time. At the time, AE was short of staff, yet with invitations for missions flowing in. We wanted to fulfil as many as we could, as we felt keenly the urgency of our task of evangelism.

Yet finally, with the kind support of Hudson Lugano, our then Social Action Director, and the permission and blessing of my Team Leader Gershon Mwiti, I was allowed to go ahead.

It was agreed that I would participate in missions each weekend and during all school holidays, and at any other point that I could possibly manage. The rest of the time, I could pursue my studies.

This was a great arrangement, for it meant that while I was studying, I could still get paid about 80% of my AE salary. This was very necessary, as with Rosemary also studying, we needed some sort of income to feed us all!

We thanked God for the ease and graciousness of how it all worked out. AE Kenya continued to do well, as John Shikuku, my assistant, did a magnificent job in holding the fort for me while I was attending classes and writing essays.

My taxi service

I was even able to earn a little extra money, through my own impromptu 'taxi' service. For I had now bought that 'KUF' pickup from my dad, at a small manageable amount. This pickup truck proved a very strategic purchase, as ILU had their student housing a little distance from the university, in Santack Estate, along the Ngong Road which was my route from Karen.

Seeing a need, I began to run a regular 'taxi' service, picking up fellow students from the Santack Estate and carrying them straight to the university. Getting to university had been a major headache for these students, as the local buses were crowded beyond belief, and in my pickup they had the luxury of benches for seats. I could take up to eight students, and their payment towards fuel costs went a long way towards also helping me with our family finances. It was just another reminder to me that God uses all things and that we were to look out for every opportunity that He brought our way.

Our time at university passed quickly, and the Lord carried us through the various trials associated with student life. In 1998 Rosemary graduated from AIU, and the following summer of 1999 I graduated from Nairobi International School of Theology. We therefore celebrated two more milestones in our lives – our Masters' degrees.

Around the same time the overseer of our denomination, Bishop Peter Sila Kiio, of the Living Word Church, requested that we should both be ordained as pastors.

'We want you to take on the job!'

12
Our Ordination, First Church and School

Don't let anyone look down on you because you are young, but set an example for the believers in speech, in conduct, in love, in faith and in purity... devote yourself to the public reading of Scripture, to preaching and to teaching. Do not neglect your gift, which was given you ... - I Timothy 4: 12 - 14

The day of our joint ordination at the Living Word Church in Pangani, Nairobi was an unforgettable milestone in our lives. It was a formal recognition that God had indeed called both of us to full-time Christian ministry. What a joyous day that was - conducted in the very same church where we had been married!

Our families and our friends were all there, and also, an unexpectedly wide range of representatives from African Enterprise. First, there were my fellow staff members from the AE Kenya office. Second, a member of AE's Kenya Board, Bishop Arthur Kitonga, attended. He was one of Kenya's prominent church leaders and founder of the Redeemed Gospel Church. Being a friend of our Bishop, he became one of the signatories on our ordination certificates. I did not know him personally at the time, but he was a friend of my dad's, and we were so glad to greet him. Thirdly, we had the international family of AE represented through Lynn Nwgbara, AE's Belgium Director, who was visiting Nairobi at the time.

Church planting in Mathare North

Of course, ordination meant that we were now able to pastor a church. Our Bishop had a special one in mind for us: the church that is located in Mathare North. It is on the edge of the tough and infamous Mathare Valley Slums. The church had been planted a year earlier.

For those who do not know Nairobi, here is a brief introduction to the horror of those slums: Mathare Valley is a long thin shanty village about five kilometres from Nairobi city centre. Mathare Valley is only 300 metres wide and two kilometres long, yet it is home to more than half a million people, packed tightly together in unspeakable conditions. It is the oldest slum in Nairobi, and sadly has just about every crime, disease, deprivation and degradation that there is. Few policemen ever dare to enter Mathare Valley. Occasionally, some well-meaning but naïve visitors from the West venture in, wanting to help; some have been known to faint at what they find.

Taking on the church in nearby Mathare North may not have been every new pastor's cup of tea, but Rosemary and I felt we were well suited for the challenge. Rosemary had grown up in the slums, and I had had a heart for ministry to the poor for many years. Also, it was during the AE mission to Mathare Valley in 1994 that I had first met Mary, who had in turn introduced me to Rosemary.

So, after prayer, we decided that the church in Mathare North was exactly where we were meant to be. We therefore accepted the Bishop's invitation and said we would take over as the pastors.

Of course, this was easier said than done, for we still lived at the University in Karen on the other side of Nairobi! Karen and Mathare

are two different worlds. But Rosemary and I had such a passion for ministry among the poor that we were determined we could make it work.

Our first job as the new pastors was simply to go and find this church. We knew it would be very different from the good, lively congregation in the Liberty cinema hall where we were currently worshipping on a Sunday. We wanted to see what the Mathare North building was like, what sort of seating it had for the congregation, if there was any sort of platform for those who took the service, and if it might even possess some sort of musical instrument for playing at worship. Of course, we didn't expect any church offices, or rooms for Sunday schools.

Our first visit remains forever vivid in my mind: there was no building at all. Rather, there was only a small old, ragged and tottering military tent! For seating they used several pieces of timber they had buried upright into the bare ground, on which they had nailed other pieces of timber to sit upon. There were no Bibles or hymn-books, but that hardly mattered, as few could read anyway. We were told that the church had once possessed a hurricane lamp, but during a prayer meeting one evening some robbers had come in and snatched it away, leaving the congregation in the total dark. Then the former pastor had left, some months ago. So now the church at Mathare North was down to between five and ten people meeting in the flimsy tent on a Sunday morning. And that was it; there was nothing else.

My tour guide that day, who was a member of the church, told me all this in a flat, almost toneless voice. It was clear that this congregation would need a lot of encouragement before we could move forward and become a thriving church. This was going to be a church re-plant!

Looking back, I thank God that He gave us Mathare North while we were still young, with the groundless optimism and energy that youth imparts. No wonder that the Bible admonishes the youth to 'bear the yoke while still young' (Lamentations 3:27): only the young have the inexperienced enthusiasm to charge ahead into situations that, to anyone older and wiser, are quite hopeless.

Rosemary and I threw ourselves into that weekend pastorate of the church with passion and determination, praying that the Lord would help us succeed. At first, we felt we were on our own, but within a few weeks, as we got to know our people, we came to realise that the congregation, though small, uneducated and timid, were also full of faith. Their love and their joy in the Lord, and their determination to be His church in that area, went far beyond their numerical strength.

Moving the Church into the tin hut

Within a very few weeks, by praying together for God's help, we managed to move out of the tent and find an abandoned tin structure that was nearby. It was an important and strategic move for the church. In the best of senses, we were not just relocating into a bigger place, but we were also, in essence, replanting the church!

But as the months went by, there is no doubt that we found pastoring that church to be very tough indeed. The sheer effort involved, just to get from Karen to Mathare Valley each weekend, was enormous. And it did not help matters that on the way to Mathare North we had to pass so many other well-kept and thriving church buildings. A little voice in our heads would ask us why on earth we had not gone to pastor one of those comfortable churches!

For there was no denying that Mathare North was not an attractive place to be. The sour stench of poverty was everywhere. There were many Sunday mornings when I was tempted to bring incense along and burn it, to freshen up the air. The only thing that stopped me was the concern that people would then think we were some sort of cult!

It also did not help that there was an open running sewer practically next to the church, full of raw, untreated sewage. One morning our young Victor walked straight into it, thinking it was stuff to play in! Rosemary rarely loses her cool, but she did that day.

At other times, both Rosemary and I could not help but ask ourselves: had we studied for years, and gained our Masters, in order to end up serving this particular church? Why had we ended up here? We could not help but feel academically over-qualified! And, experience wise, unqualified!

But God is gracious – and as we ignored our doubts, and instead laboured and ministered to the people each weekend, it began to grow.

And grow! The congregation grew until with time we were filling nearly all our seats on Sunday. It was time to move again. Anyway, the owners of the tin hut, having seen that we were putting it to good use, now wanted it back again!

So, where should we now go? We prayed and thought hard about what we were really after. It gradually dawned on us that the only way in which we could permanently impact the community was to have our own church land and building.

Buying land in Mathare North

But how could we ever afford to buy land, even in Mathare North? There was a piece of land going for Ksh 400,000 i.e., USD 4000. But, alas, our offerings each Sunday ranged only between Ksh 300 to 500 (3 to 5 USD). That was quite a big difference! We would need about a thousand times as much as a typical weekly offering!

How on earth were we to get such money? No bank would consider Mathare North Church for a loan. While in keeping with good practice we had opened a church bank account, there was next to nothing in our accounts. Everything we collected went to paying for the various basic needs for the church, the rent and electricity.

But God uses such challenging moments to build us and train us. And so, following some times of prayer and thinking, the Lord put it on Rosemary and I that as a family we could take a personal loan, in order to build the Lord's house. The leaders agreed to come alongside us and help as much as they could, i.e. out of our Sunday offerings pay for the loan. The loan was the only way that we were going to secure the church.

And so, we bought a plot of land in Mathare North. It had been used as a dumpsite for years, and was high, lumpy and very, very smelly. That probably, or divinely, was what made it affordable to us! The dumpsite then shifted to the next piece of land. In fact, our little plot of land and church would be surrounded by other dumpsites for the next 15 years.

Having purchased the land, the next challenge was to build the church. But before that, of course, we needed to clear the rubbish off the site. Hiring a tractor was out of the question, so we did it ourselves. We purchased some rakes and shovels, and, together with members of the church, we began to dig. Oh my! It was horrible, nauseating work, and the smell was quite astonishing. But on the plus side, such a humble activity helped us to bond together even closer as members of the same church. Some of us laboured during the day while some joined in after work, in evening hours. We discovered that our commitment to the project strengthened our commitment to each other. We were in this together, literally up to our knees! The memories of us working together on that dumpsite linger to this day.

And slowly, over the weeks and months, with small contributions from members, we managed to buy the materials until we had enough to build our very own tin structure.

At that point we had to bring in some proper builders, to help us construct the tin walls and put on the roof. As this was my first experience of supervising a construction, I had to learn as we went along, and learn quickly! I recall Bishop Kiio once visiting us, when the roof was being set and saying: "Stephen that roof is bent." I had not noticed that, and yet, sure enough it was. It was a good lesson: even when you have professionals, you need to supervise what they are doing.

But at that point we ran out of money, and so our roof stayed open, with big gaps, for a number of months. Young Victor, our son, did not realise that the roof was still a work-in-progress, and so happily explained to a visitor one Sunday that "our church roof is open so that God in heaven can see and hear us."

Yet, we did 'see' and 'hear' God in many ways in those early days. Only He could give us the strength and willpower we needed to keep going. For it was never easy. The floor of our church remained bare earth, and so could get very muddy when heavy rain fell outside. Then the few plastic chairs we had managed to buy were all stolen. But we solved that problem by simply bringing our own plastic chairs on a Sunday, and then taking them home again.

God's blessing

Slowly, the church progressed, and we were so happy to be in our own building! It was still surrounded by the sewer and mounds of garbage, and all a visitor would have seen was an empty tin shell of corrugated metal panels, forming a large hut on bare earth. But they were OUR corrugated panels, forming OUR hut, on OUR earth, and they mostly kept off the rain (once the roof was finished) and we could accommodate the growing number of people who were coming each weekend.

Nowadays Mathare North church numbers well over 100, and they have a new stone building under construction. But growing and maintaining a church in that kind of area will always be a problem, because once people become Christians and begin to turn their lives around, they tend to be able to get better jobs, and so buy out, rent out and or move out of the area.

Rosemary and I are so impressed with the current pastor of Mathare North, Pastor Oliver, and his wife Josephine. For they have been willing to actually live permanently in the neighbourhood, and they are considered stars in the community. Oliver was one of the teenagers in the church when Rosemary and I first arrived. We gradually mentored him into becoming a church leader, and then finally into becoming the pastor. Oliver has done stupendously well: with the support of the church, and Rosemary's passion to see a trained church leadership, he went on to gain his Diploma, BA, MA, and is now about to start on his PhD.

Another member. Johnstone, who was also a teenager when we arrived, is now one of the part-time ministers, and has completed his PhD, having begun from a BA. He also served with African Enterprise's youth programme and specifically in the Nairobi 2005 Youth Mission.

Pastor Mohamed, now pastoring Eldoret Living Word Church, was my associate pastor from those early months. He was a welder and remains one to this day. During the day he would do his welding work ,and then do church work in the evenings. I credit him a lot with the weekly momentum of keeping our church going, given his proximity to it. Emily, his wife, worked so hard with Rosemary to launch the Tumaini Academy for those slum children. It has grown beyond recognition, and to date has helped hundreds of children in Mathare North.

Social needs

There is something about a slum which draws you in. At least, it did to us. As the church gained root in Mathare North, and we got to know our church people better, we became increasingly aware of the needs of both them and the community. Each Sunday Rosemary would look into the dull, pinched faces of the children, and remember her own childhood of ignorance and some neglect. Finally, she decided she simply had to do something. So she determined that she would start a little school. We had no resources and no money, but that did not stop Rosemary.

First of all, she needed classrooms. So, she hunted around until she found some large bits of torn cardboard. She and her recruits dragged these into our church hut and used them to divide up some of the church space into classrooms.

Then she needed teachers. She recruited Mrs Mohamed (my associate minister's wife) as the first teacher and ultimately the Head Mistress. They visited around until they found other local women in Mathare North who could read a little bit. They agreed to come and help her teach the youngsters. Among these was Polly who has since then (2003 to date 2020) served as a teacher and current early childhood education Head Mistress. Maggie – Margaret Wairimu became the 'chef' – cooking for the children – porridge. All these were serving as volunteers. Rosemary and I made arrangements for Pastor Mohamed to build some seats for the kids.

Books and paper were the next challenge, and this really was a challenge, because the local parents could not even afford the subsidised monthly Ksh 300 ($3) that we were requesting them to contribute – way below the cost of lunch and porridge per month. Still we gathered what books and paper we could, and did our best.

Yet the plight of those children preyed on our minds. This was the time when AIDS was so rampant, and so many adults in Nairobi were dying. They were leaving behind 'families' with no living adult left in them, and so young children were now the 'head' and taking care of siblings barely younger than themselves. These child-headed families had no income, and so they would then be evicted from their rented shanty homes. The children would then end up on the streets of Mathare North or further out into the city, with nothing and no one to help them.

Those children haunted Rosemary, for she knew from personal

experience the horrors of being left as an orphan in the slums. She went through a very haunting season over this, for many months, because working with the slum orphans kept bringing back to her so many horrific memories of her own very harsh childhood. Her book Against all Odds: Rising from a humble beginning – captures her story.

All this time. I was also working full-time again for AE, and Rosemary was busy with our growing family of now two lively children (our daughter Joy having been born in 2001). Each weekend we pastored the church in Mathare. Given the itinerant nature of AE's evangelistic work, Rosemary was from time to time on her own with our other leaders in Mathare, running the church. Members of the church also joined us from time to time in AE's work, including, in the course of time. sponsoring youths to join our FoxFires youth mentorship programme.

Amsterdam 2000

Then in the summer of 2000 a momentous event changed everything in our lives. It began in Amsterdam, of all places. There was a great international conference, Amsterdam 2000, which the Billy Graham Evangelistic Association were holding for evangelists from all around the world. The BGEA wanted to bring them together for mutual learning and encouragement. It was to be held in Amsterdam in late July/early August of that year.

By then, my recruiter, mentor and former AE Director for Kenya, Gershon Mwiti, was in America, doing his doctorate. Standing in for him was our Finance Manager, Jason Nyaga, as acting Director for AE Kenya, and so it was agreed that Jason and I should attend Amsterdam 2000.

As Jason had some AE meetings to attend in Wittenberg, Germany before Amsterdam 2000, he went on ahead, and I flew to Amsterdam to meet him in late July. It was my first trip to Europe, and my hopes were high at what Jason and I would find there.

Amsterdam 2000 was beyond anything we had seen before. Slightly over 10,000 international evangelists, all in one conference centre! It was tremendous, encouraging and so inspiring to meet and share the experiences of evangelists worldwide, who shared the same passion for the Gospel as we did. Christianity Today documented it as one of the most worldwide multicultural gatherings up to that point: (https://www.christianitytoday.com/ct/2000/julyweb-only/32.0d.html).

Then – out of the blue – tragedy struck. Jason fell ill. I visited him at his bedside since he could not make it for sessions on the final two to three days of the eight day congress.

But alas, on the final day of the Congress , he died! Bishop Kitonga and Bishop Anondo, both of them AE Kenya's board members present at the conference, were of great support to me and the Kenyan delegation. The doctors thought that the severe chill he had picked up in Wittenberg a few weeks before may have triggered some sort of pneumonia, and thus his collapse.

There followed the shock and trauma of getting his body safely back to Nairobi. His wife Casty and the kids were great friends of our ministry, and Rosemary and other team members back in Nairobi did their best to comfort them. Jason was so well loved, that it was a tough and sad time for all of us in AE Kenya and the entire partnership of AE.

I flew home in a very sombre state of mind . Amsterdam 2000's conclusion had been heartbreaking. I met with Casty and explained the circumstances surrounding her husband's demise. Though relatively older than us, their five children were still young. We spent time mourning with them.

Having laid Jason to rest, we had to begin the long search for a new head of AE in Kenya. Finally, the day came when the National Board arrived at our Karen offices. We seated them in the main side hall downstairs to discuss the future of AE Kenya. Dr George Wanjau was our Chairman (and former Moderator of the Presbyterian Church in Kenya) and so he was leading the process. On our staff side, Janet Mworia our accountant and Julia Ochieng, our Social Action director, were in attendance. Meanwhile, I was seated in my little office upstairs, busy working.

Called to new responsibilities

Then suddenly there was a soft call 'Steve! Steve!' That was Janet calling me. Was it an expense that I needed to account for? I went out into the corridor, but she was not outside of her office. Instead, she was standing at the foot of the stairs, looking up at me. 'Steve, come down, the Board wants to see you.'

Now I did not like the sound of this. What had I done wrong? This was cause for more anxiety than having to go through finances with Janet and account for funds! Slowly I went down the stairs, putting on my best 'business look', unsure of what the Board could possibly summon me for. I looked to Janet for some sort of hint, but her face was a blank. She said again, flatly: 'The Board wants to talk to you.'

'Why?' I whispered urgently. 'What for?'

But there was no answer from Janet. She just gave me her 'no nonsense administrative' look, and turned and walked back towards the Board Room. Reluctantly, I followed, my mind racing. I kept trying to think of what wrong I might have unknowingly committed following Jason's death. Was there some sort of administrative procedure of which I had fallen foul?

It was hard to step into that room, as I had never even met the Board in a formal seating before. They invited me to take a seat that they had placed in the middle of the room, directly in front of them all. This looked serious! But I choked down my apprehension and kept my best cool 'business look' firmly in place.

"Steve," one Board member said, "You know why we are here today – the loss of Jason has been a big shock and grief to us all. But we must accept it and move forward. We have discussed the future and have decided that we will appoint you to act as National Team Leader for the next six months. At the end of that time, we will review the situation and decide the best way forward."

That was it. There was no dialogue or argument among them, they all seem resolved that this was what AE Kenya must now do, to keep moving forward. Jason's death had been a blow; but we had to keep the forward charge to win Kenya's cities for Jesus. Like an army, we had to press on forward!

I was stunned. I was beyond speech. I had never entertained such an idea. I loved my preaching and setting up missions. Moving on up in the organisation had never crossed my mind. Until that day, I had never even met the Kenyan board. But this was an impromptu appointing, following a colleague's demise, so the promotion was a sober one, with no rejoicing. I also knew that I had to be faithful to discern what a valued colleague who had died had been seeking to achieve!

I went home to Rosemary and startled her with the news as well. We prayed about it, and about all the implications it would mean for our lives. My local preaching would be greatly curtailed. I could no longer adequately pastor the church in the slums, as I would be travelling so much, right across Africa, to liaise with the other AE teams. There would be endless administration and people management to bear. And I would not be able to carry my weight at home; Rosemary would have a lot more of the raising of our two children to do.

And yet, and yet, as we prayed, the old promises kept coming back to me: God had called me to go from 'the reached' to 'the unreached', from 'the possible' to 'the impossible'... well, here were new frontiers and new vistas I had never dreamed of. But this seemed to be the next step that I was to take.

My father had also known the Nyaga's, having taught at Daystar with Casty. He was both stunned by Jason's passing, and stunned at my being asked to take on the baton as AE Kenya's National Director. I was 34 years old , still relatively young. He shook his head in wonder and amazement as he thought back to our old arguments about me wanting to be a preacher. His son might well have been called to travel and preach, but I was anything but an itinerant, wandering street preacher!

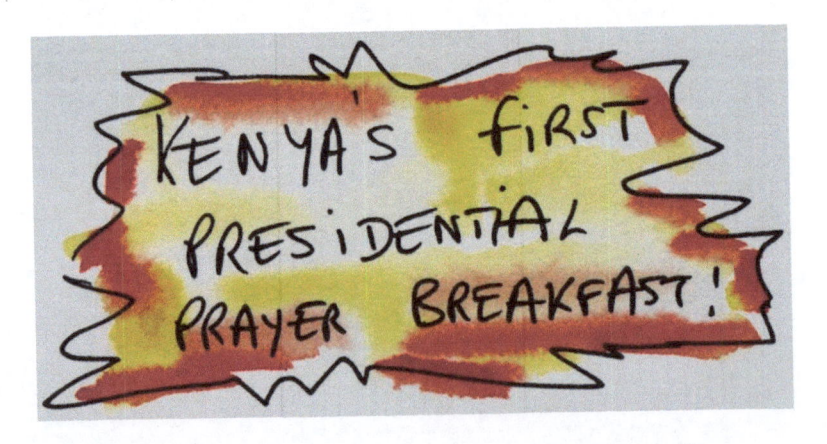

*'Into this political maelstrom, my team and I
launched the National Prayer Breakfast in Parliament!'*

13
Team Leader for Kenya

*'I urge that first of all prayer be made for
all people for kings and all those in authority,
that we may live peaceful and quiet lives. . .'
- 1 Timothy 2:1-2*

My first six months as Acting National Director of AE Kenya (2000-2001) flew by, and soon the Board had assembled once again, back in the main meeting room of our AE offices in Karen. A little while later they called for me to come in and join them. They had placed the chair for me in the centre of the room, facing them all. Again, I put on my best 'business' face, and awaited their decision.

"Stephen," said Dr Wanjau, the chair (and former Moderator of Presbyterian Church of East Africa), "the AE Board has decided unanimously that we should confirm your appointment, and that we would like you to become the permanent National Director of African Enterprise Kenya."

As I accepted, I could not but marvel at how God's promise that He would send me from the 'reached to the unreached', and from the 'possible to the impossible' was working out. In the weeks and months that followed, there was so much to learn, and I was so grateful to God for the presence of my colleagues on the team. Janet Mworia, our Accountant and Administrator, had served with AE for much longer than me, and was an invaluable source of knowledge, experience and wisdom. She helped me a great deal. John Shikuku, who had deputised for me in missions, now assumed the permanent role of 'Missions Director.' Julia Ochieng, our Social Action Director, was also on hand with all her community experience to give me a hand in engaging with communities that we were seeking to transform with the Gospel.

As for me, well, I was now carrying the permanent responsibility for a national team. Here indeed were new vistas, and many new challenges for ministry! As the leader of AE Kenya, I soon realised that I could see things from a different, wider, perspective. The Lord was challenging me, and I realised that while I had done mass evangelism and spoken at innumerable open-air meetings, there were still 'unreached groups' whom I had never yet touched.

These were the movers and the shakers in each country, each city: the political leaders, the market-place leaders. These people would never turn out for public rallies, popularly known as 'crusades.' If you wanted to reach them, you have to plan very carefully… they are rich and elusive! So, I prayed and wondered what to do.

Washington DC

About this time Michael Cassidy sent me to represent him in a conference in Washington DC. As I was the youngest national director that AE had at the time (I was only 34) he was discipling me and also opening new opportunities for me. His kindness and generosity of spirit were a boundless encouragement.

The conference in Washington DC was being run by the chaplain to the US Senate, the Rev Dr Lloyd Ogilvie. He wanted to let us, as select delegates from around the world, see how ministry worked out on Capitol Hill. So, as well as meeting in the magnificent National Presbyterian Church (NPC) in downtown Washington, we also met on Capitol Hill itself, so that we could have a sense of how ministry among political and top government leaders happens. Very illuminating! David Carpenter from Memorial Drive Presbyterian Church in Houston, a friend from a visit he had made to Kenya, and later to become a board member of African Enterprise USA, was also a delegate.

I listened carefully to all that I heard. For months I had been thinking and praying about our national leadership of Kenya, and praying and wondering how they might be reached. This was providentially very, very timely in affirming and opening my eyes to possibilities with top leadership ministry. Back home in Nairobi, and using what I learned at that conference, but bearing in mind Kenyan culture, I made up my mind what I would do.

Once back in Nairobi, through my role as Kenya's Team Leader for AE, I formed the Nairobi Leadership Initiative. It was to aim at bringing the Good News to our political, business and government leaders, while calling them towards servant-value-based leadership. I then invited the heads of various Christian organisations to a forum for the purpose of planning this mission, geared to the leaders of Kenya.

This would not be a mission in any stadium or hall, it would not have any singing, it would not have any loud preaching. Not at all. Instead, we were going to target Nairobi's politicians, the police, the military, and the professionals. We had the same passion to share with them the Gospel, but we were going to use very different tactics. With these sorts of people, we needed to channel our passion for the Gospel in a very different way. The lesson from Washington had gone firmly into my head: 'They will never come to you – you must go to them, and in a way in which they feel comfortable accepting you.'

Nairobi Leadership Initiative

As I was still young, with boundless optimism, I aimed high: the first 'event' of the newly formed Nairobi Leadership Initiative was going to be with the President of Kenya and members of his government! Once I had them on board, the rest would follow. The plan was that once we could engage and win-over the President and his top government ministers, we would then proceed to other levels of top leadership: in the Military, Police, Business community, etc. Each meeting would address the 'top people' in a way that they could easily understand and with which they would feel comfortable.

So, this was certainly putting the principle of 'from the possible to the impossible' into action! I prayed to the Lord to teach me, and to stop me from making a fool of AE or seeming to make a fool of the Gospel.

By now it was 2003, and Kenya had been going through a difficult time. President Daniel Moi's government had become tyrannical, and people had been 'disappearing' off the streets. It was even rumoured that there were torture chambers somewhere in the city - the notorious 'Nyayo Chambers'. People had been very frightened, angry, and feeling helpless.

For months the tensions had gone on, until at the end of 2002, a new, third, President of Kenya, had taken office: Mwai Kibaki. The transfer of power happened in a public event at Uhuru Park. In that event President Moi, as outgoing President, apologised to the Nation and to anyone he might have offended. The event was very acrimonious, with some publicly abusing the outgoing President.

President Kibaki, having been in an accident in the final stage of the campaign, was in a wheelchair that came to be known as the 'wheel barrow'! That he won against Moi and the ruling Party's candidate Uhuru Kenyatta, was in itself a miracle. So, the whole issue of leadership, and what it should now look like, especially as Moi's had leaned towards being more dictatorial than democratic in its final stages, was something very much on the public mind.

The National Prayer Breakfast

It was into this political maelstrom that my team and I proposed to launch a National Prayer Breakfast in Parliament. I had consulted and prayed with my national Board, and we felt that God was calling us to do this, despite all the difficulties. After all, from the possible to the impossible... and what could be more unlikely than that? But it was the perfect time: we had a new President, so now was the time of fresh opportunity and new beginnings, with the old regime gone. The new regime needed our prayerful support and was open to new ideas.

I began by first forming a team that consisted of leaders of various Nairobi-based Christian organisations. They were to act as our National Leadership Initiative and National Prayer Breakfast Steering Committee. The response was heartening, for we were joined by World Vision, Bible League, and Campus Crusade, among others. They were all very positive and came on board with enthusiasm and promises of on-going prayer.

We then drew up a formal invitation that we could send to members of Parliament on behalf of the Nairobi Leadership Initiative. Next, I approached the few members of Parliament whom I already knew, the first two being the Hon Samuel Poghisio, who had once been my lecturer at Daystar, and who was a friend of my dad's, and also the Hon Joseph Nyaga, who was already known to be a Christian in Parliament.

At this point we made a happy discovery: there was already a fledgling Prayer Breakfast Group in Nairobi! The Hon Samuel Poghisio told us about them and arranged for me to attend one of their meetings at the Boulevard Hotel. Unknown to us, they had also long wanted to conduct a National Prayer Breakfast in Kenya. I found that so interesting - to learn that sometimes, when God gives you an idea, however unique you think it is; in fact, it is not. He has given someone else a similar idea, and He obviously expects you all to be mature enough to reach out and work together on the same idea.

So I reached out to this other Prayer Breakfast Group at the Boulevard Hotel. It was led by an American missionary, Sam Owen. He had had hands-on experience of working on the Washington Prayer Breakfast Movement in the States, and so was very helpful. Although AE's long-term plan was not to aim only at the political leaders, we were all agreed that our first effort together should be for politicians. After all, we all agreed with the African proverb which runs: 'when the fish begins going bad, it begins with the head'!

There was another advantage to having found the Boulevard group. Whereas my planning group was composed mainly of leaders from Christian agencies, this other group, led by Sam Owen, consisted of mainly former government and business leaders. These included Eliud Mahihu (once Provincial Commissioner during Kenya's first President Jomo Kenyatta's era) and James Mathenge from that era as well. Dr James Mageria (current Karen Hospital Chairman) was also part of this group. Having gone to school with his son and having served as Chairman for the Daystar board, I had a good connection with him. The two groups together strengthened and complimented each other.

We had soon put together a programme, and approached Ole Kaparo, the then Speaker of the National Assembly. We explained our concept for the events, and the fact that Parliament should take a leading role. It all sounded a very different approach to them, since they had expected that church leaders would want to lead any church-related function.

Kenyan Parliament

Ultimately, the Members of Parliament were galvanised by the Speaker and members of Parliament (early adopters) such as Samuel Poghisio, David Musila, Kalonzo Musyoka and Joseph Nyaga. Then the Members of Parliament not only said yes, but even contributed from their own pockets, as opposed to using national public funds to support the event.

Our Prayer Breakfast Steering Committee (the Boulevard group and our National Leadership Initiative group) rejoiced at the news – this thing was really going to happen!

We had also approached various churches in Nairobi, asking for their financial support. Slowly, two of them decided to come along, but they were very hesitant. Many other churches hung back for a while longer, uncertain as to how this would work out. But as the weeks went by and the National Prayer Breakfast gathered interest and support, at last many more church leaders decided that it would work. Then, at the last moment, many of them wanted to get involved! In fact, we ended up with a crisis, because suddenly so many leading church leaders wanted to be part of the event – including being in attendance. But we had limited places for church leaders, since the main focus was on the political leaders and market place leaders.

I will never forget the day when senior leaders invited me for a breakfast meeting in one of the restaurants to discuss the National Prayer Breakfast. Unknown to me, they had got wind that I was the main link for churches to the event. They rounded on me, their main line of attack being: "How can you plan such a major national event without us being on board and how can we miss out from such a national event?"

Their grilling was so intense that both I and a colleague who accompanied me never even ate the breakfast they set before us. Instead, they had us for breakfast! That grilling wasn't all a loss, though, because out of that meeting some then decided to contribute financially to the event!

Meanwhile, I was quickly learning that when you decide to set up and launch a major event, be prepared! The more attention your event attracts, the more problems it will also attract.

Somehow, by God's mercy, it all came together, and on Saturday 31st May 2003 we conducted Kenya's first National Prayer Breakfast at the Intercontinental Hotel. We chose our date strategically, to be the last Saturday of May. The reason? 1st June is Kenya's Independence Day.

The event was therefore positioned in order that we could engage with public thought on what values our nation should aspire to hold. Calling to mind the price paid by our freedom fighters, we set a sober mood, wanting to challenge the nation to adapt an ethical and value-based leadership.

Strategically, we also planned the event in such a way that Members of Parliament played the main role during the Breakfast, including the reading of Scriptures, the sharing of testimonies and prayers. By so doing, other Members of Parliament were affirmed and encouraged to discover that there were fellow godly men and women among their top leadership roles.

Senior military and members of the judiciary were also involved in the programme, further enhancing the visibility for godly leadership in other circles of leadership. The Honorable Kalonzo Musyoka, the then Minister for Foreign Affairs, became the event's emcee. President Yakubu Gowon, retired President of Nigeria, and a Christian leader, was our speaker for the event.

President Mwai Kibaki

Our newly-elected President Mwai Kibaki was a man of few words, but he also gave his supporting remarks, which went a long way in affirming the event. Meanwhile, in the background, the National Leadership Initiative committee and African Enterprise were also honoured by being mentioned by the emcee for our behind-the-scenes role in serving as the Planning Committee.

The National Prayer Breakfast has continued to run annually without fail every year since 2003. It was during the 2019 National Prayer Breakfast that President Uhuru Kenyatta reached out to his political rival and leader of the opposition, Raila Odinga. The reconciliation between the two led to peace, the country having been in conflict since the contested 2017 elections. This pact has been lauded internationally, including the two having been accorded a chance to address the United States National Prayer Breakfast luncheon event.

In reaching out to political and leading market place leaders, there is a parallel in Mark chapter 2, where, when Zacchaeus upon encountering Jesus, is immediately seen inviting his fellow tax collectors to come and meet Jesus in his house. The tax collectors related to each other. In the same way, politicians relate to each other. In another way, sadly, they can also often be seen as under suspicion and not to be wholly trusted… but Jesus loves them, and they need to hear His message. So, Christian politicians and market place leaders can show by their lives what it means to be a Christian in politics and public service, and how to work for the good of their country.

My prayer is that one day, in every Parliament across Africa, we will have a 'church' (defined in Matthew 18:20 as 'where two or three meet in His name') made up of the country's Christian leaders, and that that 'church in Parliament' will pray for their country and each other, and also become witnesses for Christ to their country. They have unique leverage at that level.

Leadership forums

Our behind-the-scenes experience at planning and launching the first National Prayer Breakfast event gave us the necessary impetus we needed in order to reach out to the next levels of leadership.

Building on that momentum and the publicity gained, we proceeded to conduct similar leadership events for the Police, the Business community, Women Leaders, Student Leaders, Youth and the Military. The events were conducted in various leading restaurants in the city, with the exception of the Military event, which happened within their Nairobi Department of Defence (DOD) barracks.

The success and challenges entailed in running these events were a major learning curve for us. But that was not the end, as other cities began inviting us to conduct similar Leadership forums. That meant that over the following three years we had similar leadership events in Mombasa, Nyeri, Nakuru, Embu and Kisumu. These were all Top Leadership encounter events, where we challenged the top leadership in government, business and the private sector to move towards a more godly form of leadership. This was true mission to the leadership of our country: we were going to them in their own 'territories', and not expecting them to leave their comfort zone and come to a Christian meeting.

We soon found that by offering what we called 'leadership forums', we got a good response. We would approach the leaders of a particular sector and say: 'Do you want to offer corrupt leadership, or learn the principles of servant leadership, where you work for common good, and not for your own gain?' People were intrigued and came along, and slowly we began to change their mindset of what a successful leader should look like. It should be one of service, not of dominance and greed.

Of course, we hit massive problems at times. We were dealing with some very powerful, very manipulative people, and of course it did not always work out as we had hoped. But slowly, slowly, we were helping to establish an on-going Christian presence in the very heart of the leadership of Kenya.

What struck us, as we had spent so many years doing exuberant missions, was just how different the strategy is when you are reaching out to the leadership of a country. You catch the attention of leaders one by one, not by throwing out a large net and hauling them in! The whole process is far more diplomatic, more sophisticated, and requires a lot more money and self-confidence. At that level, people come through to Christ one-by-one, and not in a group. It can take months, years, of patient and persistent witnessing and prayer for them.

We did find that we could also begin to use Christian politicians and policemen to 'catch' each other, by encouraging them to share their stories with their colleagues.

We also found that even the Muslims were interested in our leadership forums. We invited them all to come along, explaining that no matter what they thought of Christianity, they would still be learning good principles of leadership. We could see that many of those who came were deeply challenged by what they heard, and deeply moved.

One such encounter was in the 2004 Mombasa Leadership Forum, where a uniformed services event was held following my presentation on servant leadership, based on Jesus' leadership style. Two Muslim Prison officers approached me. They shared with me their excitement at the lessons they had learned from the event, and how they had never seen that type of leadership before. They were conversant only with the 'big man' type of leadership. This was transformative for them, in terms of leadership, and I believe a seed was sown into their faith journey.

*'In my preaching that morning, I brought
in the challenge to Africa's leadership.'*

14
National Prayer Breakfast for South Sudan

"If a man's gift is leadership, let him govern diligently." - Romans 12:8

Meanwhile, 2003 marked another major landmark in our lives.

Rosemary and I were still pastoring the church in Mathare North, where the plight of the street orphans had always troubled us. We had tried to help some of them through an AE sponsored project, but the children had not responded well to the rather impersonal approach this necessitated.

Opening our home to orphans

So, by 2003 we were wondering if the Lord wasn't challenging us to do something personally for those kids.

By now, Rosemary and I had bought a small patch of land in Ngong on the outskirts of Nairobi (about 10 kilometres from Karen, and about 38 kilometres from Mathare North). On it we had slowly built a little house for ourselves. It was a simple house of brick and mortar. Members of our church had come out to help us do some of the construction (mixing concrete, fetching water etc) in keeping with the team-work spirit we had all shared when we built the church structure. By the time we had moved into the house it still had no plastered rooms except the kids' room, and there was no piped water, and no electricity. But at least it was ours!

Now we decided that we would attempt to use our 'possible' to attempt another 'impossible': providing a home and care for a number of needy orphans. We were already both working full-time and raising our own two young children (Victor 6, and Joy 2). It wasn't going to be easy!

So, we opened our small three-bedroomed house and took in two children. And then we took in another two children. Then some more arrived, until we had eight children. Life was becoming a bit hectic!

But we coped. Our strategy was to take in only very young orphans, within the same age brackets as Victor and Joy (6-2). This way we aimed at keeping things not too erratic for our children. In addition, we took in another couple, Pastor Ngaba and Edith, who were serving with us in the Mathare church. They came to live with us so that they could help us by serving as additional parents to the children.

This was all in keeping with our commitment to offer the children some parental figures, as well as a secure home, food, clothing, education, spiritual nurture and medical care. Basically, whatever we could afford for our own children, we wanted the other children to have. That was our policy, and one that we felt the Lord had impressed on us. So, such equality became our standard, from our very first engagement with vulnerable and orphaned children.

Creating a family feel

It was a challenging project and approach. But this concept of creating a family feel for these vulnerable children had been firmly implanted in us by an experience that Rosemary and I had had in 1994, during our courtship. It was during one of our African Enterprise outreaches in the notorious slums of Kibera, when we had ministered to four young street boys who then became believers through our mission.

With the help of Joseph Mulinge, who was also on the staff of AE Kenya, we did all we could to disciple those boys. Having grown up as street children, they were quite wild. Then we came up with what we thought was the 'brilliant' idea of getting them out of the slums by relocating them to Kasarani-Mwiki, a neighbourhood where Rosemary was living while at university.

So we rented a small iron-sheeted room for the four boys, bought them mattresses, food, a cooking pot, and moved them into their new home. I now had two good reasons to visit Kasarani-Mwiki: to see Rosemary, and to see our four boys.

But to our shock, when I dropped in one day after only two or three weeks, I found that they had run away! When we finally found them again, back in the streets a few weeks later, we asked what had gone wrong.

They were sheepish and thanked us for all we had done. But they went on to explain that they had simply been too lonely in the new place. They told us that they had missed their 'family' i.e. friends who were in the streets. In the new place, there was no such 'family.' And so, they had left.

This lesson stayed with us. Street children do not just need a house or food. They also need family, people they can talk to and feel comfortable with, and to whom they feel a sense of belonging. Home is where your family is. No wonder the Bible says that 'God sets the lonely in families' (Psalm 68:6).

And so, when we began taking orphans into our home all those years later, we thought back to the lessons learned with those four boys. It shaped our approach to our engagement with the children whom we sought to rescue. We would aim at giving them not just stuff, but a family experience with a father and mother figure in addition to other basic necessities – food, school, spiritual nurture and medical care. It was to be a home and not an orphanage!

Reaching out to the leadership

Back at AE Kenya, from 2003 onwards, I grew more and more committed to 'leadership outreach' until it became a real priority in my ministry. The reason was simple: I had done mass evangelism for years, and yet had reached very few, if any, top leaders through that method.

Coupled with that, Kenya and many African nations had governance issues that needed urgent attention. At one point, I had worked out that between 2003-2005 there were 27 African nations that were either starting political tensions and conflicts, or in the middle of political tensions and conflicts, or were slowly coming out of the same.

Add onto that were the constant struggles with corruption and other social economic issues that had their roots in poor political leadership. It was a critical time in Africa's history; her leaders badly needed Christian standards. They needed a moral compass to guide them in the choices that they made, because they were affecting the lives of millions of people. This made me realise that the need for 'leadership outreach' in Africa had become critical. I had also increasingly been exposed to Michael Cassidy's priority on leadership in his and AE's approach to missions.

For the next few years, leadership outreach therefore became a priority in AE Kenya's evangelistic strategy. In addition to our traditional evangelism, we also planned and carried out leadership outreach in cities right across Kenya. We were so hungry to reach these leaders, to learn the best ways in which to approach them and invite them to leadership events where they could meet other Christian leaders and have an opportunity to 'catch' the Gospel from them.

Leadership outreach to South Sudan

Then in 2006 the way opened for us to take all that we had learned and hold a leadership outreach in the new country of South

Sudan. What a tremendous opportunity! The region of Southern Sudan had been through some very tough years, as it began to split from the North of the country, and my efforts to get there had been disappointed, with visas denied by the Northern Khartoum based Islamic regime. But in January of 2005 the Comprehensive Peace Agreement was signed, followed a few months later, in July of 2005, with autonomy for South Sudan. As that signing was being deliberated, I sensed strongly that this would be the critical point for us to begin our entry into South Sudan. Change was in the wind and we had to be ready to step in at the earliest opportunity.

My team and I came up with the plan to get into South Sudan and contact the church leaders in Juba, the soon-to-be capital of South Sudan. Our AE Kenya team decided to try and finance our trip on what money we had from within the country. I went around challenging churches in Kenya on the fact that as South Sudan's immediate neighbour, we had to do something ourselves, as opposed to waiting for churches and people of goodwill in the West to step in. We had to lead the way! But CITAM (Christ Is The Answer Ministries)was, to my recollection, the only church that answered our call, although others sent verbal encouragement.

In mid-2006 I flew to Juba. We could only manage to get my flight ticket, and so contrary to our usual plan, I travelled alone. From the 'known' to the 'unknown' – the 'known' in this case was Across, a Christian agency that I knew from Kenya and which also worked in South Sudan. They received me well and gave me an orientation into life in South Sudan. Their Director, then Antony Poggo, had been to Daystar to talk about South Sudan. Charles Ramadhan, their logistics officer, became a good friend and my chauffeur around Juba. They graciously made arrangements for me to meet, as arranged, with the church leaders of the city. I pitched my message to them very simply:

"You have come through many years of hardship, but now you are starting to do a great thing: you are beginning as a new nation!

This is a critical time for you! Most if not all our African countries, when they threw off their colonial masters and gained independence, wasted so much time in turning against each other, and in fighting constantly among themselves. Each new country wasted millions of dollars and ruined many millions of lives in doing that.

"So my challenge to you, as the church leaders of Juba, is to help your people now by reaching out to your leadership in this city, in this country. AE Kenya has learned strategies for how to reach city and national leaders with the Gospel, and we want to join with you now to do the same for South Sudan. Help us to organise a leadership outreach initiative."

In a number of settings, the church leaders of Juba listened attentively to me. The late Bishop Michael Lughal, a senior Anglican minister in the city, was among those that took to heart that message, and we developed a very good friendship from that point.

Through the church leaders, I then secured an appointment to meet with James Wani Igga, the Vice President of South Sudan. This was a great step forward! I had met national leaders in public before, but this meeting would be in his office. I had hoped that some of the church leaders would come with me, but on the day of the appointment, I found myself all alone.

Persuading the Vice President

I stepped into the Vice President's office and was astonished by the sheer size of it. It was enormous! And Wani Igga, seated at the very end of this long classroom-sized office was all imposing and very commanding. "What do you want?" he asked crisply. I could see that I might get a brief hearing, but nothing more, unless I could catch his attention.

So, walking towards him, taking a deep breath and getting seated as close to him as I could get, I began: "I am a leader and a preacher from Kenya, and I believe that following the peace-deal, South Sudan has a critical window of opportunity before it. What happens next will be largely up to the leadership of this country, and I want to challenge them to make the most of this unique opportunity to set South Sudan upon the right path."

I repeated my message about how other African countries had got into too much internal fighting. "South Sudan can easily go the same way of fighting and corruption. Do you leaders really want that for your country? Or do you want to take the better route of modelling yourselves on the Christian model of servant leadership, and not always doing things in the selfish African way?"

Then I told him about the leadership outreach programme we had run all over Kenya, from the Presidential Prayer Breakfast downwards! Whether it was that, or whether he simply liked the idea, I do not know, but before I left his office, I had won his powerful support. I could sense the Lord's presence had been right there as I shared with him.

The Vice President was true to his word. He went on to back us, all the way into organising and holding a Presidential Prayer Breakfast for South Sudan! Having got the green light from the Vice-President, I left South Sudan confident that I could speak of the event as 'being in the making'.

Not long after, I was back in Juba, this time with William Muchiri, our AE Kenya Social Action Director, for further planning work. The Juba Episcopal Cathedral had become one of our main allies, and the Lord used one of their members in an interesting way to meet our transport need.

We had had to use taxis, motorbikes and bicycles for some of the planning work. We had even done a good amount of walking and running, just to get around Juba. There were many times when I would arrive at Parliament all dusty, and had to dust off my shoes before going into the offices. My appearance was critical, since at this stage the subordinate staff took me as also a Member of Parliament, due to my frequent visits, and my proximity with the MPs. I had therefore to look the part, and be smartly dressed.

Then came the Sunday when I was ministering at the Cathedral in Juba, at the invitation of the Provost. He had known African Enterprise since the 1980s, through Bishop Festo Kivengere's visits to Juba. In my preaching that morning, I brought in the challenge to Africa's leadership. After the service I was shaking hands outside, when one smartly dressed gentleman came over to greet me. He was interested to know more about our mission and the Prayer Breakfast that we were working on.

The gentleman then explained to me that he worked in high levels, close to the President. He then instructed his driver to carry me around for the next couple of days. Any time we needed a car, I was to call him and he would make arrangements. That was a miracle indeed from above, and an answer to our real need!

It was during this visit that we firmed up a planning committee in Parliament. With directives from the Vice-President, a team was built with the indefatigable Honorable Jimmy Wongo as chairman. Paul Bonju, serving then as Parliament's Communications Director, took on the role of planning secretary and Mr Modesto, Parliament's Legal advisor, became our advisor.

Given the economic challenges in South Sudan at the time, raising any funds for our work in Juba was a major challenge. But African Enterprise's resources were not much better: our Board had not anticipated that this leadership mission would happen when it did, so we had not set aside funds for it yet. But I had wanted to grab this opportunity to get into South Sudan, and so I just had to raise most of the resources from churches in Kenya and (to a small extent) South Sudan.

Here Hon Jimmy Wongo came in very handy. One day we literally went door to door, as he used all his influence to raise funds for this initiative. He approached fellow Members of Parliament, banks, parastatals and businesses. And through him, the Lord rewarded our efforts. With a man like Jimmy Wongo, sold to a cause and committed to see it happen through the mobilisation of local resources - all things are possible!

Later support from our African Enterprise Australian office helped us in flying in the various speakers from Kenya into South Sudan during the actual Prayer Breakfast. Otherwise, most of the food for the National Prayer Breakfast, as well as for the other Leadership events, including the Uniformed services (Military, Police, Prisons), Student Leaders, Women Leaders and the Clergy, was provided by the Christians in Juba – a monumental effort, considering the impoverishment of the country.

National Prayer Breakfast in South Sudan

June 11th 2007 was the day set for the first-ever National Prayer Breakfast for the Parliament of South Sudan, and we were well prepared. We held it right inside the Parliament buildings, being the only building in town that could host and secure such a high-profile event. The Parliament building in itself was a tale of what South Sudan had been through: the building had many holes from being hit by explosives from the Northern army.

For speakers, I had brought over a scratch team, including Gershon Mwiti, now back from his doctorate in the States. His senior uniformed services credentials were handy in this context, where most of the leaders were top former and serving military leaders.

I had also brought along, as the guest speaker, General Lazarus Sumbeywo, who had been the lead negotiator for the peace-deal that brokered peace between the Arab Islamic Sudan and South Sudan. General Sumbeywo, himself a professed Christian, was also highly regarded by the emerging South Sudan leadership. Simba Rashe from Zimbabwe, a former AE Kenya Foxfire, William Muchiri and Helen, an intern from Australia, were also present to give support.

The President, Mr Salva Kiir Mayardit, was there, along with James Wani Igga, the Vice President, and a good representation of members of Parliament, military leaders and government leaders. Leading clergy and NGO leaders were also in attendance, among them World Vision and Norwegian Church Aid and Across that had joined up in financially contributing to the event.

The Honorable Jimmy Wongo, as emcee for the day, took to the stage and gave a background to the event. As the Coordinator (or vision bearer) I then followed, to give comments and to set the stage for the event. Unlike our First Prayer Breakfast in Kenya where a number of the Kenyan MPs had already been to the United States National Prayer President, I had to be the one to provide the tempo for this first one in South Sudan. I pitched my challenge as a call to the Members of Parliament and all national leaders of this new nation (though it was not until 2011 that South Sudan finally became self-governing) to reconsider their ideas of what proper leadership should be at this critical time in their history.

The challenge of 'Servant Leadership'

I painted a picture of what servant leadership was about: responsible caring for the people, and of making decisions that would help to achieve the most good. I then contrasted that with what too much leadership in Africa had become: dictatorships that made decisions that only served those in power. I said that leadership is about being called to serve, not to be served. I urged that as leaders we should advance the nation forward into the future, and not backwards.

I then proceeded to invite our Guest Speaker, General Sumbeywo, who shared his hopes and aspirations for the new nation. From his position as a peace-mediator, his message resonated deep into the lives of the Members of Parliament. Many of them had been to the bush in the struggle, and so would have still harboured vengefulness. His call to balance action with the Christian grace of forgiveness and diligence to build the nation was well received.

Vice-President Wani Igga then came on, and in his characteristic charismatic way he gave his added call for good leadership. I was to later learn during my PhD data collection that he had written some books on leadership.

President Salva Kiir then came on stage to make a response. Though usually a man of few words, he added to the message by calling on the leadership to abstain from corruption. However, he made the audience laugh by relating how being 'black' is equated to being evil and corrupt. Though he remained focussed on those of us who were present, it was clear he was directing that remark to foreign powers that have a stereotype view of Africa's leadership as being all evil. The senior clergy, including the Head of the Roman Catholic church, Pentecostal churches and my friend Bishop Michael Lughal then led in closing prayers.

In a few hours the event was over, and it had gone very well. We got good feedback from a number of those who attended. At the end of the event, right there in Parliament, someone came up and asked me: 'When is the next event?' That was a good question! As I reflected on how to answer him, it dawned on me that my work with the leadership was event-oriented. But the Lord had seemed to be saying to me: "It will take more than events to transform those in leadership" It calls for a process, an ongoing programme focused on leadership to achieve transformation in their leadership ethos.

Cabinet Minister baptised

Some other memorable feedback came from the Minister for Communications in the new government, who came up to us afterwards, wanting to talk.

"I want those servant leadership values you guys spoke about."

He proceeded to explain how, long ago as a youngster he had been a Christian. "I then went to the bush, took up my gun and lost Jesus in the struggle for our nation's freedoms. You have reminded me of my history. I want to be a Christian again." Bishop Michael Lughal prayed for him, then became the person to follow him up.

In the course of time that cabinet minister requested to be baptised. We set the day for the baptism, and when news of it got out, it caused a bit of a sensation in government circles. It was most unusual for adult men to be baptised in Sudan, and it was unheard of for a Minister of State to be baptised!

So, on the day, a great number of his colleagues came along to the Episcopal Cathedral, including Salva Kiir, the President of South Sudan himself! There was great curiosity and sincere interest, and absolutely no mocking; they were genuinely wanting to understand what their colleague was doing, and why it was so important to him. The Secretary General of the Sudan People's Liberation Movement (SPLM) party echoed what this meant to many when he got up to speak at the baptism: "I don't go to church, but because of this our father – being baptised – I came to church today." That cabinet minister like Zacchaeus was bringing his kind to Jesus!

Afterwards, the AE team and I could only praise God and marvel at the doors He had opened for us in South Sudan. Our strategic outreach to the leadership had resulted in our 'reaching' one cabinet minister who in turn had captured the interest of other cabinet ministers, who were then challenged by the Gospel, in a setting in which they felt comfortable. It was, once again, the model found in the New Testament story of Zacchaeus, where he comes in, and then brings along his own type who normally are so hard to reach.

A programme needed

A few weeks later, back in Nairobi, I kept thinking about the amazing trip to Sudan. What had we learned that we could put into practise for more leadership outreach?

The question from that one participant then came back to me: "When is the next event? I felt the Lord's conviction afresh to the effect that: "You are still operating as an evangelist, but you cannot change leaders and bring lasting transformation through occasional outreach meetings. You need to set up on-going programmes."

The more I thought about this, the more the truth of it grew on me. But what would such an on-going programme look like? What should it include if it was to be of any real help to a leader in modern-day Africa?

That opened up a whole new range of questions! What, exactly, made a leader different from other people? What particular qualities did they tend to have, and what qualities should they also have? What motivated them? What should motivate them? What values did they have, and what values should they have?

And I realised that I needed to find out more about the modern leaders of Africa. How did they function in the maelstrom of modern African politics, against a constant background of on-going national challenges? What were their real strengths, and weaknesses? What were the real temptations for them, and what values could help them become the leaders that our nations so badly needed? I did not really know, and yet I needed to find out, if I was to have any long-term success in reaching out to them with the Gospel and playing a role in bringing about lasting national transformation.

Doing more research

In 2011, the very year that South Sudan became self-governing I would go back to South Sudan to find out. This was part of my PhD research at Biola University, California. That question that day inside the South Sudan Parliament had led me searching down this path. I interviewed 29 members of the South Sudan Parliament. This included even the Vice President. This time he graciously invited me to his residence for the interview – a much less imposing setting.

Among the questions I wrestled over with these leaders were: 'What values have you internalised, and where did they come from? Did they come down to you from a Christian heritage? Or were they from the context of traditional African culture? How do traditional values such as sharing and communal life impact your generosity as a leader? How do you live up to that giving culture and how do you service it? What values came down to you by having a chief's family heritage? What values prepared you for your present leadership? Where would you place values such as integrity and faithfulness?

I was trying to look at what makes a leader in modern Africa, and to do some sort of critical analysis. I wanted to find their strengths, and the gaps in their values, so that we could help them. I was heartened to hear that the church and biblical values were widely known and appreciated, if perhaps not so often put into practise! For full findings of that research read my book Values and Motivations for Leadership: A focus on the Legislators of the first South Sudan Legislative Assembly.

My aim was to build a model of what a modern African leader, infused with Christian leadership values should look like. I wanted to begin by thinking through what good leadership models might already exist and be authentic in an African cultural setting. Secondly, I wanted to bring in the biblical aspect, and finally to also borrow from the Western leadership models but build them on an African platform.

That question led me down a new path, as Rosemary on the other hand was equally being led to pursue her PhD in Leadership and Administration in Higher Education. This was 2008 and another big milestone in our lives was beckoning: it was time to take time out, and to do our doctorates.

'Life in California was not quite what we had expected...'

15
Doing our Doctorates at Biola University

Remember how the Lord your God led you all the way in the wilderness these ... years, to humble and test you in order to know what was in your heart, whether or not you would keep his commands. - Deuteronomy 8:2

In 2008 I resigned as AE Kenya Team Leader, after 16 years with African Enterprise.

It was not an easy decision to make, because AE had given me the most fulfilling and productive years of my life. But after 16 years, I was 41 years old, and I needed a change. I felt that I had given all that I had to give, and that it was time for me to have a break from constant ministry.

I wanted some space to evaluate what I had been doing, and to learn more. I was still passionate for evangelism, but I wanted to better understand the mindset of modern African leadership, and how we might reach them with the Gospel. There had hardly been any time to really critically think over this challenge in recent years, between the frenetic pace of missions, and the growing number of orphans in our care.

By now, Rosemary and I and the two children had moved out of our little house, so that the 14 orphans would become bonded and established with the 'house parents' instead. We had a name for this home now, ByGrace, and we loved them all, but did not want them to get too personally attached to us. The reason was that we had set our minds on going for further studies, and we did not want the orphans to experience another great emotional loss in their lives. They had been through enough already.

Rosemary and I had looked around the various universities in Nairobi, but none of them offered a doctorate in our areas of interest. In my case, it was Intercultural Studies, with a focus on political leadership. Rosemary was interested in the Administration of Higher Education in Christian Universities. So, we prayed as to where we should both go.

A number of our Christian Kenyan friends had gone to America, some to Fuller Seminary, to do post-graduate studies. The idea that we might do that, too, began to grow in us. That would be an opportunity to learn, and one that would enrich us for the rest of our lives.

Which university?

At first, I felt drawn to Fuller University, but my approach to the university came to nothing. It was like beating on a brick wall, really uncanny, because they have many overseas students – including at that point my predecessor, Gershon Mwiti, who had just completed his doctorate from there. But for some reason, I had no feedback from them at all. (Later, I learned the reason. I had given my application forms to a member of the Fuller faculty when he had visited Nairobi. When he returned to California, he forgot to submit my application to the admissions office.)

Meanwhile, we had begun to consider Biola University instead, and the doors flew open so fast that Rosemary and I realised the obvious: that the Lord wanted us to go to Biola!

To begin with, Rosemary had discovered that she could get a scholarship to pursue her PhD at Biola's Talbot School of Theology.

As for me, well I had had a 'divine pointer' to Biola in 2007, when I flew to Dallas for some scheduled AE ministry. A good friend of AE, Dan Dill, asked if I could squeeze in a visit to Los Angeles, in order to visit the headquarters of his ministry, Life Lift. We had already partnered with Dan and Life Lift in order to sink a number of water wells in Kenya and Congo DRC.

(The water well that Life Lift sunk in Suswa (Kenya) went on to play a critical role for good in tribal tensions in Kenya. The well had given such relief to the area that it had led to a peace-pact between the Kikuyu and the Maasai. So strong was this pact that even when Kenya fell into the post-elections violence of 2008, the Masaai community in Suswa refused the temptation to fight the Kikuyu. Instead, they said "we made a pact by sharing the water, and we cannot break it now." The harmony that the well had brought meant that this was one of the places in Kenya where the two tribes didn't fight, in spite of their close proximity. Given the political climate at the time, this saved many lives!)

Going back to 2007 and Dallas, Dan's invitation to visit him in LA was simply beyond me; I had to explain that there were no funds for the extra leg of the trip. But Dan was not discouraged, and ever generous, simply organised my ticket himself!

It's a miracle!

When I finally reached LA, the first place that Dan took me was to Biola University. It is on the edge of Los Angeles county, and has a beautiful, tree-lined campus of 95 acres, with gracious red-brick buildings and gently curving roads. Although already a qualified pilot, Dan was studying there himself at the time, pursuing a Master of Arts degree in Apologetics at Biola. Dan took me to the Intercultural department, where I met Dr Rich Starcher, who had been a missionary in Kenya, and who had taught at the university where Rosemary was now teaching. In fact, he had been Rosemary's mentor!

Dr Starcher then introduced me to Dr Marla Campbell, who was the Dean of the School of Intercultural Studies. I had a chance to share with them both about my passion for outreach to leadership. I explained that this was why I wanted to pursue research at Biola, in particular focussing on Africa's political leadership, with South Sudan as a case study.

There and then, I was offered an 80% tuition scholarship!

I can still see Dan's beaming face once we had left the Intercultural department. "This is a miracle! A miracle!" he kept exclaiming. "This does not happen to everyone - don't get the idea that this is just the fast way that Americans do things. Not at all."

So, I returned to Kenya sure beyond any doubt that the Intercultural Studies department of Biola University was the place for me to pursue my PhD.

But how?

There remained the problem of how to finance the trip. This was going to be a big step in faith. America was much more expensive than Kenya, and we often struggled to meet the bills in Kenya!

We began by holding five harambees (fund-raising events). Even our beloved church members in Mathare North, a good number of whom led very humble lives in the slums, were determined to help their pastor go study in the USA. I was deeply moved by their generosity and their faith in me. We immediately assured them, during the church

Harambee, that they had bonded with us by their love. We would return to them, upon completing our studies. We would not desert them, by staying on in the USA. Their willingness to help us overwhelmed us. One very poor lady went around the slum door to door, selling bits of scrap paper, just to help raise a few more shillings to fund us. This was like the Macedonians, of whom Paul writes: *And now, brothers and sisters, we want you to know about the grace that God has given the Macedonian churches. 2 In the midst of a very severe trial, their overflowing joy and their extreme poverty welled up in rich generosity. 3 For I testify that they gave as much as they were able, and even beyond their ability. Entirely on their own, 4 they urgently pleaded with us for the privilege of sharing in this service to the Lord's people. (2 Corinthians 8:1-4)*

Some commentators say that the 'extreme poverty' denoted here is a 'down-to-the-depth poverty', a real rock-bottom poverty. That is what many of our congregants were like, and yet, like the Macedonians, they were pleading with us for the opportunity to give!

The Board of AE Kenya, led by the chairman, Isaiah Kimani, was equally very supportive. They organised a fund-raising function for us which, as I had resigned, quickly became a farewell-to-African-Enterprise party. Having spent 16 years with AE, it was a very moving event for me.

Our family conducted a similar fund-raising event, and so did my contemporaries, my fellow preachers. We then conducted a similar event at the Africa International University (AIU – then NEGST) and invited our friends at large. The goodwill experienced from all these groups and friends was overwhelming.

And so the money flowed in, until in all we had about $15,000 dollars. I then took out 50% of my pension, as permitted by Kenyan law, and used this to add another $2,000, to make a total of $17,000 for our use in the USA. In Kenya in 2008, $17,000 looked like a fortune! But we knew that once we got to California, the money would be stretched. While Rosemary had a scholarship to cover her fees, we had to pay 20 per cent for my first semester's tuition bills right away, as well as meeting our living expenses.

Goodbye to Kenya

Finally, in July of 2008, we said a loving good-bye to our other 14 kids, and flew to California, taking our two young children, Victor and Joy, with us. Leaving the rest of them behind was tough. Even though we had brought in house parents, and they knew they were secure, it still felt for some of the kids as if they were being twice orphaned. We felt their pain, and totally understood. But it was necessary that we should go, and somehow, we felt that in the larger scheme of things, it was for their good also that we should leave.

We landed at Lax (Los Angeles International Airport) and found our friend Dan Dill, like an angel on an assignment, waiting for us at the arrivals gate. He drove us straight to Biola, where we had already been warned that there was no apartment currently available for us on campus. We would have to arrange our own accommodation for a while. But Dan had already got to work on the problem, and took us on to Corona to meet some Kenyan friends of his, Patrick and Lydia Kimani. Their two kids, Baraka (boy) and Imani (girl) were nearly Victor and Joy's age.

Patrick and Joy were to become our 'Kenyan family' away from home, and for the next five years we celebrated Thanksgiving and Christmas holidays with them. Meanwhile, that first day they welcomed us so warmly that we felt immediately at home. Over the following week they gave us an intensive orientation course into life in America from an African's perspective. That included showing us where we could buy 'Spanish' food that was at least similar to some Kenyan foods, such as corn flour for cooking Ugali, one of our common Kenyan dishes.

Meeting some angels

All too soon we had to leave our new-found friends and begin another important orientation – settling into our new life at Biola as 'educational migrants.' The Kimanis drove us to La Mirada, where another angel, Judy Wills, was waiting to help us with this.

Rosemary had first met Judy in a previous short visit to Biola, when she had come over for some modular courses. Dr Obi, one of the lecturers, had introduced them on the campus as Judy was walking past. The following Sunday, Rosemary had agreed to go to church with some Biola students, but when she arrived on campus, she could not find them. So she had wandered around the neighbourhood for a bit, looking for some church she could attend on her own. Rosemary had stumbled upon Granada Heights Friends Church, so she wandered inside, and met some very friendly 'welcomers' at the reception area. One of these was Judy Wills, who greeted Rosemary as if she had been specifically expecting her. She was a firm friend from that moment onwards.

When we arrived as a family, Mama Judy, as we got to calling her (Grandma Judy for our kids), had already located an apartment for us to rent. It was in an apartment house off-campus, and it was perfectly situated: not too far from Biola, not too far from a primary school (Garden Hill Academy) for Joy, and not too far from a middle school, (Hutchinson) for Victor. Mama Judy had done an amazing job!

As if that were not enough, Mama Judy had then mobilised an army of well-wishers, many of them members of Granada Heights, to donate household items such as beds, couches, and kitchen ware. She had managed to equip that apartment with all of the necessary basics our family could possibly need. We will forever remain grateful to God for Mama Judy's unique heart and serving spirit. We learned later that many years before, she had been of similar support to Dr Orbie, who was now serving as a lecturer at Talbort, Biola. She has a heart of gold!

We then began to explore our new 'home' of Southern California. Biola, La Mirada (where we would live) and Los Angeles were certainly a change of scene from Nairobi!

Biola University is on the edge of Los Angeles county, with a beautiful campus, well-equipped classrooms and a magnificent library. It is a beautiful university, comfortable middle-class America at its best. It could not have been more different from the slums of Mathare North or our simple house in Ngong Hills.

Our first challenge was transport. Public transport around California is very poor, and it was immediately obvious that we would need a car. Once school opened, Joy needed to be taken to school, but even just shopping and church would need transport. Luckily, we had come a month early, before schools opened, and we had time to sort ourselves out. In the meantime, Mama Judy became our chauffeur and transport manager.

Ramshackle 1

Our search for a car took us to one of Biola's graduating students, who wanted to sell his 20-year-old Toyota Corolla. We blinked when we first saw it – it was in different colours! That became our famous car on campus, and we named it Ramshackle 1. Over the years, as various parts of the car had been damaged, they had simply been replaced rather than repaired, to save on labour costs. A further saving had been made by not bothering to match the colour of the added parts to the colour of the original car. So, for example, Ramshackle 1 had a side bumper that was red, while the car was grey.

It was a car to behold, but during our time in the USA, five years in total, it never once broke down on us. Many times we would be driving the freeways and see newer cars broken down by the side of the road, but our Ramshackle 1 just kept going. I thanked God for our miracle car!

But to drive it, I had first to take the California State driving test. In America, of course, they drive on the 'wrong side of the road' i.e. the right-hand side, while in Kenya as a former British colony, we drive on the left – and believe it's the right side to drive!

Driving the American way took some getting used to! I failed the driving test three times before finally getting it on the 4th attempt. It was very humiliating. Victor, who knew I had driven for over 10 years in Kenya, kept laughing and wondering why dad was now failing this test. My driving instructor was very patient, and told me he had helped Kenyans before; it was our bad driving style that was the problem! Slowly he helped cure me of several bad habits, and at last I had my American licence and could stay on the right side of the road.

Money worries

Fuelling the car wasn't the only bill we now had to worry about. There was rent at $1400 per month (which reduced a couple of months later to $1200, once we had moved into the Biola apartment). We had, in addition to my 20% tuition fee, to also pay out $1000 ($500 each) per semester for insurances. This amount was so huge that we only paid it since it was demanded of us by the school's policy. Sadly, we couldn't afford to pay the same for our children, and we felt very uncomfortable about that, but there was nothing we could do. Finally, buying food and paying for electricity, gas and water took up a big part of our monthly bills. Our hoard of $17,000 was diminishing pretty fast.

Meanwhile, we were faced with the biggest new challenge of all: semester had begun!

The academic demands of Biola are very high. As neither of us had done academic study for more than seven years, we needed to shift mental gears fast! The studies were very stressful because of the sheer volume of work required: lectures to attend, book lists to get through, and a seemingly endless array of essays to produce. The culture in the classrooms was also very different from Kenya, far more assertive and challenging.

I was soon swamped, especially at the thought that there were two full years of this to survive, before I even started the research and writing of my thesis in my area of interest. I was also disoriented by such a total change in my daily work, in the culture, and increasingly worried about our finances. At first I struggled to concentrate and keep up with the classes. How were we to survive four years of this?

Secondly, I was 20 years older than many of the students, and from such a totally different culture, that I found it hard at first to relate to them. This was especially true as becoming a student again was having a big, unexpected effect upon my own self-identity.

For years I had been National Director of AE Kenya, and had built up a wide network of good Christian friends and contacts that stretched across Nairobi and beyond. I was well-respected within my circle, and as my position was senior within AE, of course many doors would open for me. That was simply how it was, and that was who I was.

Who am I, anyway?

Now of course, on Biola campus, none of that mattered to anybody. At Biola, like any foreigner and newcomer, I was without friends, without any network to relate to. Now I was just Stephen, a penniless older student driving an old car, surrounded by comfortable middle-class Americans, many in their early 20s. Nobody was unkind, they were just oblivious, busy with their own lives.

I wanted to reach out to the students and members of faculty around me and make new friends. But there was simply no time to 'hang out' on campus and socialise; we had two young children to collect from school and to care for.

The fast-paced American culture was also at play here. On Sundays we would often find ourselves among the last to leave church after the service. It was just that we had never been to church for anything as short as a one and a half-hour service before! We felt that we had just arrived, and everybody was going home. Back in Kenya, we had been used to being in church all morning, and then staying on in the afternoon for leadership meetings.

Happily, Granada Heights church also had a group called the Genesis group, and they held hour-long classes which ran between the various Sunday services. Anita and Conrad, the leaders, made us feel very welcome to their participatory discussions of Christian issues. This one-hour class, added to the one and a half hours of service, was not much compared to Kenyan standards, but at least it made us feel like we had been to church at all!

On Sunday afternoons we then proceeded to visit the Kenyan Lifeline fellowship which ran from 3 to 6pm. Friends of ours back in Kenya, Nelson and Ruth Kuria, had told us their daughter was near Biola, and when we had met Cynthia, she had in turn introduced us to Paster Moses Ndereba of the fellowship.

The Kenyan fellowship was so culturally different from our morning American church experience! After the service, we had plenty of time to fellowship and socialise over tea.

We simply loved it – it nourished the African part of us, and we would go home feeling we had really connected with others and had had a proper Kenyan Sunday. The Kenyan fellowship and Genesis therefore became our main places for socialising.

Besides this Sunday socialising, the rest of our week was packed full with classes, the library, dropping off and picking up Joy, and study at home while keeping an eye on the children. Cooking also became one of our shared chores, since unlike in Kenya, we did not have a house help. Here it would have been a luxury beyond our imaging! Also, it was not in keeping with the culture here. When we had first arrived, Victor had often jokingly asked: 'Where are my maids!' But he was rapidly learning that in America you do your own chores, and pick up after yourself! Good training indeed.

Silence from AE Monrovia

An added source of stress was the fact that I was aware that African Enterprise had an office in downtown Los Angeles, in Monrovia. I had done ministry trips in the past for African Enterprise in the USA, and so of course had been welcomed there. But having resigned from AE, I was now here in a totally different status. I sympathised with the donkey that carried Jesus into Jerusalem: on its trip back home, it must have wondered where all the crowds had gone, and what had happened to the cloaks it had been given to walk on!

There was now no AE for me in this strange land. I could not turn to them for companionship and support. The office in Monrovia existed solely to raise financial resources for the evangelists and communities back in Africa. I was therefore wary of going there, in case they felt that I was after some financial support for myself, when their job as a charity was to raise money for AE work in Africa. It was obvious that AE had no obligations to me now, as a just a foreign student.

However, I was deeply emotionally attached to AE. I had served them for 16 years, and it felt so strange not to associate with them at all now. So I decided to pay just one brief visit to the Monrovian office, to greet an old friend, Malcolm Graham. I also offered to be available if they needed someone to speak about AE. This seemed an excellent idea to me, as I could well have helped them with meetings. After all, in the past they had paid to fly me over to America to speak, and now I was here already, and willing to do it for free.

But although Malcolm and his staff were as kind and friendly as ever, that was it. It was perhaps an AE policy here that anyone now outside of AE's support raising structure should not be used. Even when later I organised for Michael Cassidy and Stephen Lungu to come to Biola to speak, there was no engagement at all with the AE office in Monrovia. In their eyes, I was yesterday's man. And, that was who I was indeed – and I had to slowly learn to accept it! God seemed to have put a veil between AE and me.

All in all, as that first semester went on, soon Rosemary and I were wondering what on earth we had done. We had left secure and respected positions in Nairobi, where we had many friends. Here we were struggling with our studies, struggling with culture shock, we were lonely, we were alarmingly short of money, and we had nobody at all to look to for solace.

Our children, being children and oblivious of our woes, were excited about their schools and making new friends. However, their English had an accent and local kids had teased them: "where on earth do you come from?" Victor was then 12 years old, and so conscious of peer pressure that for six months he refused to speak to us in Kiswahili, in an effort to clean up his English. This really troubled us. Daily life with the family got challenged; we were increasingly unhappy.

Visiting food banks

Came the seventh month, and we ran out of money. We saw it coming; but were totally helpless. After paying for some up-front necessary costs like the car, and keeping our spending to the bare minimum, we were still in trouble: the $17,000 had drained away at about 1,700 per month.

We had done our best and avoided buying so many things, even food. There were many times I would take victor to the mall for the food, and he would try and help by putting food into the trolley. Most of these items I put back straight back onto the shelves. Victor gave me some strange looks – why was his dad acting so weird?

Thank God, by now we had discovered that our Granada Heights church had a food bank. So, from time to time we would pick up some canned food stuff. Fellow students would also inform us when they knew of a church that was giving out food. And we would go along and join the queue with the others, some well-dressed, and some homeless vagrants. We were hungry.

One day when we were once again running very low, I recalled that a church nearby was feeding recent emigrants (refugees) and the homeless that afternoon. I rushed straight over and waited for some unsold bread from local restaurants the day before.

As I arrived, I ran into the man who had told me about this church: he was wheelchair bound and lived off handouts because of his poverty, but he was a cheerful Christian all the same. I remember thinking: he and I are in the same league now – we are both beggars.

Unexpectedly, that made me smile: my former AE Kenyan colleague John Shikuku (now late) had had a saying: "Good news is one beggar telling another beggar where to get food." Then the words hurt: I had never dreamed that that would become literally true in my life.

For some reason, this church food bank had attracted many people that afternoon, and their unwashed poverty and misery were so stark. I looked round at them all: their need was so obvious that I was reminded of the African famine seasons, where pictures of starving children and the malnourished become front page. That prompted my memories of having dished out food to others at the Nairobi Show ground as camp coordinator, following the 2008 post-election violence, which was still fresh in my memory.

I stood there waiting for my stale bread and wondered what was happening to me.

I had come to America to do my doctorate so that I could better serve God among the leadership of Africa. But now here I was, just as desperate for food as these desperate people from the underside of American life.

That afternoon, I felt the psychological strain becoming almost too great to bear. A year or so before I had been working with church and mission leaders and from time to time engaging with Members of Parliament and Cabinet Ministers in Kenya, and more so (south) Sudan. Now I was in America and reduced to sharing bread with homeless and hopeless humanity in California.

Visits back home

I felt like I had fallen off the edge of my known universe! What had become of me? Who was I? I felt my whole self-identity crumbling. The present was becoming a total horror, and the future was a mountain which my mind said we would never be able to climb. I could feel depression nibling at the edges of my mind.

Finally, we had to face it: we were not going to survive without some regular funds coming in. We had heard that many students / emigrants in the States go onto the black market, but I did not want to do that. We had prayed to God that we would be faithful and strong, but here we were, both succumbing to despair.

Fortunately, by then the summer of 2009 was approaching, and we had tickets to go home for a while. We somehow managed to do this each summer, and for several very good reasons.

First of all, we wanted to stay in contact with our 14 children we had left back in Nairobi. We did not want them to feel twice orphaned. Our taking them into our family had caught the attention of several Americans and slowly a little support group for our ByGrace Home project was growing. It would, eventually, become ByGrace Trust, with summer trips of US supporters going to Kenya to help out with the children. Two good friends in California, Lori Clock (now Fox) and Dee Hamilton, were full of enthusiasm for ByGrace. They kept things going for us in the US, and still do, today.

Beside Lori and Dee, some others had come over on working trips for our ByGrace Home. This included an organisation called Foundation for Peace, a team from Granada Heights Church, and two teams from Biola's SMU (Student Missionary Society). These teams were able to include the price of our tickets into their fund-raising drive, as we were the mission leaders and the mission would not happen without us. We thanked God for this gracious provision.

Secondly, we wanted to keep Victor and Joy connected with Kenya. We knew that if we did not make these annual trips home, it would be very difficult for them to return after five years in California.

But even now, looking back, I wonder how we ever made the four trips in the five years that we were there. It was all miraculous provision.

We returned from that 2009 summer trip to Kenya to face some stark reality: we urgently needed money. Once back at Biola, I therefore began an earnest hunt for a part-time student job. Any job would do.

As students, our foreign students visa (popularly known as F1) only permitted us to work in the School. This was after 9/11, when the terrorists who had crashed into the Twin Towers had been officially registered in one college studying one thing, while learning to fly planes in another institution. USA authorities had therefore instituted stringent laws on foreign students including – 'work only within the school you are attending.'

Job hunting

This meant that where once we could have used our credentials to seek ministerial work in local church settings, now we could not. We had to work on campus.

But jobs were very few, with many foreign students after each one. It was barely a year since the global recessions had hit, the most severe economic and financial meltdown since the Great Depression.

So while I applied for everything from cleaning classrooms and offices to doing telephone fund-raising for the university, nothing worked out.

Finally, I learned that the Campus Safety department needed students to work along the Campus police in enforcing security. Mmmm . . . history seemed to be repeating itself! Years ago, back in Embu, I had asked the police, as my very last option, if I could work for them.

They had turned me down. Now – over 20 years later, and nearly 7,000 miles from Embu, I was asking the American Campus police if I could work for them. And given the economic circumstances, I wasn't sure if they would turn me down as well!

Captain Alvarez and one of his colleagues interviewed me. They were at first confused: my background as a preacher, missions organizer, National Director etc didn't make sense here. So then I mentioned my past membership as a Scout, hoping that that might help!

One of them peered at me in friendly amazement. "Do you really want to be a security guard? Aren't you a bit over-qualified? And hey, do you know how unpopular security guards are? We have to put parking fines on cars that are in the wrong place – man, that does not make you popular! You will be shouted at!"

I left the interview feeling very anxious. I knew I was older than the other candidates, with none of the right background. But I needed that job!

Campus safety department

When a few days later word came that I had got it, I could feel the waves of relief sweeping over me. After going through the Campus Safety cadet training course, which covered security, safety, as well as some basic military codes, I was ready to begin work.

The walkie-talkie, belt, torch and keys would be assigned when reporting for shifts.

The night shifts (10pm to 4am) were considered the worst, and therefore were avoided by most. On the contrary, those were the best shifts for me, as I could work on my PhD during the day. Also, I preferred to keep a low profile, feeling uncomfortable to be seen as 'the African Campus Safety adult student walking around with teenagers – keeping the peace' guy.

And so, I joined the night shift. Our code name was Zebra. I was

Zebra 17. There were 16 Zebra's ahead of me. Considering I came from Kenya, I guessed Zebra was good choice for our code name. I was Buffalo (Mbogo) and I was Zebra!

And so began an intense, sleep-deprived existence that lasted for many months. Each night, all night, I walked the streets on campus, patrolling different parts as assigned of those 95 acres of lecture halls and on campus apartments. Since my family was in one of those on-campus apartments, I comforted myself that at least I was watching and securing my own family as well.

I would finish at 4am, go to the office to sign out and return the torch, belt and keys. I'd rush to the apartment and sleep from around 5 to around 7 am. At 7am I would rise to take Joy to school. Sometimes a neighbour would assist with that. Then I came back and slept another hour. Then I started the day's study work for my doctorate. One of us picked up the kids from school, we did more studies and preparation of supper. I would then aim at sleeping again from 7 until 9. If I did not sleep then, I would have the most difficult night ahead, fighting off sleep!

Since some of our seminars happened 5 to 8 pm, it was inevitable that some of the nights were doomed to be tough. At those time I would try and opt for the early morning, 6 to 10am shift. This entailed unlocking about 60 doors on campus (I counted them), my fingers aching by the time I was done. That shift also involved carrying out parking enforcements, and that was not easy!

Earnings from all this? I earned $8 dollars an hour for 20 hours a week, or $660 a month. Rosemary also found a part-time job in the library, where as a writing consultant she proof-read and guided foreign students in writing their papers – for 10 hours a week at $10 per hour. For that she earned $400 per month. That took us nearly to the $1200 rent. Not yet fully there but somehow, we kept going on.

Making new friends

On the plus side, the work brought me into daily companionable contact with the police and my fellow cadets. Those six hours every night became opportunities for us to share at length, and great friendships slowly began. My loneliness on campus began to fade, as we cadets used talking as a mean to stay awake and alert.

In time, some of the officers and cadets went on to became part of the ByGrace (our children's work back in Kenya) support team. Some of those friendships forged in the fiery furnace of that year are still going strong today. In fact, Officer Jason, who was in charge of placement (kind of HR) at Campus safety, ended up doing most of the ground work for the registration of ByGrace Trust in the USA and becoming its first chairman!

In the meantime, I patrolled the streets each night. There was a lot of time to do soul searching and prayer as I walked around that campus for six hours in the dark. Top of my mind was: "Why, Lord, why?" Why was this such a difficult time for our family? I tried to understand what was happening. Why were we being so severely tested, so totally crushed economically? I knew that God had brought us here, but why was it so hard staying here? What was the point of all this suffering, after so much blessing of our work back in Kenya?

As the months went by, I began to discern that God was saying to me, and by extension to us as a family: I am training you to be a leader at the next level, and this is an intensive course in servant leadership! And of course, servant leadership involves being servant of all…

It certainly was an intensive course. And we nearly crashed out. The crises came in the summer of the third year, when we finally hit rock bottom with finance. Even with both of us working part-time and living off food banks, we simply could not pay the bills.

Summoned to the Accounts department

Finally, the axe fell: I was summoned into the Accounts office at Biola. I was informed that the computer had alerted them that we had not paid our medical insurance for two semesters. The Director for Finance was irritated with our apparent negligence and had summoned me. Without funds for the medical insurance, the computerized system would not recognize us as students. The summons that day was therefore to bring to my attention the fact that we were being terminated.

It was a very low moment. I sat there, abashed, in front of the Director, who looked both concerned and yet very firm. It reminded me of the days in Kangaru when students would be thrown out of our school for not having paid school fees. They had left feeling crushed, knowing that this was the end of their studies and their dreams for a good future. I had always been blessed with a dad who paid my school fees, but he was not here now, and I felt as crushed as those students back home had been.

The Director saw my misery and revealed that she had a deeply caring side. She gently asked me: "How did you get yourself into this situation; leaving your home country without enough funds and without a plan on how you will pay your bills?" To that I had an answer. I introduced myself to her, told her about my calling and my work back in Kenya. I told her about my work with AE in mission to leadership, and of the eventual need for us to undertake PhD programmes in fields not available in our home country . . . and about the five fundraising events raising the $17,000. What a pitiful amount that seemed now, sitting in California!

She seemed convinced of my sincerity and tried to think of a solution. "Why don't you remain, while your wife returns to Kenya with the children?" But I made it clear that that was not an option for us: "We can only stay here together or else all go back together." We were in this together. What I didn't tell her was the fact that

Rosemary's PhD was more important than mine, as it was absolutely required of her career as a lecturer at university level.

In my case as a preacher, a doctorate was not a 'do or die' qualification. But, as the head of the family I had to make these decisions. We would stick together as a family. On a different day I would have also told her our name "Mbogo" meant buffalo, and buffalos stay together! But that day the mood was too grave for that.

The Director closed our interview by encouraging me to think of a solution, and to do it fast. But she also prayed for me and my wife and children. And as I stood to leave, she reached into her purse and gave me $20 to go buy some food for the children. I walked out thanking God under my breath. I felt like someone who had just been reprieved from the death penalty – but wondered for how long?

We prayed and we prayed. Nothing happened. So the next day I shared with Rosemary a thought that had been growing in my mind for some time: "Is God real or just a figment of our imagination?" For where was God in all this? Why was He apparently not answering any of our prayers? Had it just been an accident that we had been exposed to Christianity back in Kenya, and so had become Christians? Had we been deluding ourselves all these years? Was Anybody really out there?

I was startled by Rosemary's roar of laughter. Then she said - "I got to that point several months ago. I have been waiting for you to get to arrive there as well." It was my turn to burst out laughing loudly.

Silver linings

Having laughed our hearts out, somehow eased off the tension. And a strange sort of peace seemed to settle upon us. We were at ground zero, waiting to be thrown off our doctorate degrees. We could do no more. Yet it seemed as if somehow, God had been waiting for us to get to this point of acknowledging our total defeat. I think

He eavesdropped on our conversation that day, and possibly laughed to see that we had now become doubters, wondering where He had gone.

The peace we felt seemed an affirmation we were not alone and had not been alone. Quietly, we reflected on the silver linings that had gleamed from time to time through our dark cloud. We recalled people who had at times quite miraculously refreshed us. Some had dropped food or gifts to make up for our shortfalls.

Ivan Chung, who was heading Biola's foreign students department was one of this. From time to time he had surprised us with a parcel of food or some cash. Dr Starcher and others had equally from time to time surprised us with gifts. Our Genesis group had been there for us from time to time.

There had been the lady who anonymously dropped some shopping to us every month for a period of about a year. Not knowing who she was at first, we simply named the food that arrived on our doorstep as "angels' food." This was because 'angel' was part of the name of some of the food she left us. We later learned she was Anita Finley, and a member of Granada Heights. Her husband taught at Biola.

Then there had been some men at the Kenyan fellowship who had been made aware of our need by the Pastor. They had held a collection for us twice, which helped a lot towards family expenses.

These memories, and the feelings of having to constantly stand in front of people as one needing help – had made me feel ashamed and embarrassed. I did not want to be a burden on anyone. I felt like a specimen out on display! All I could do was to draw comfort from St Paul's words "God has displayed us . . . last of all . . . at the end of the procession . . . to the whole universe, to angels as well as to human beings" we have been made a spectacle for all to see (I Corinthians 4.9).

But as Rosemary and I looked back on it all, there had been assurance in many ways, both spectacular and non-spectacular, that the silver lining had been there. There were many glimpses of kindness and encouragement. Some of our fellow students, who were also going through financial trials, did their best to cheer us on. Even the Head of Finance, who should have pulled the plug, had also, in a way, rallied around us!

Apartment manager

Then came a good breakthrough: early in 2010 our apartment manager was graduating, and recommended me as his replacement. It was a caretaker's job, but in keeping with our school's 'value added job's titles' – it was referred to as the Apartment Manager. Delighted, I went for the interview at the Student Housing offices and passed. Rather than pay direct cash, the job gave us a $300 discount on rent. What a blessing! The rent was now covered. We were slowly getting there. Having hit rock bottom, we were slowly moving in the only possible direction – and thankfully not in the direction of Kenya just yet! We need to accomplish our studies first.

The job meant ensuring the apartment compound was in order, washing machines were clean and functional and there was swimming safety for our apartment's children. Thankfully, I had very good and un-complicated neighbours – most of them were pastors (well, they too can be complex at times). In fact around that time we even began a fellowship where we would get together to sing and enjoy a joint meal. And at last we had something to sing about: our rent was covered. There still only remained the big challenge of finding enough money for our food and insurances (health and car), fuel and books.

One day, during one of my Campus Safety day shifts, a gentleman approached me and jumped onto my golf-cart. He asked me to give him a ride towards the main administration block. (When you did the day shifts, you were often given a golf cart to help you get around more swiftly.).

I was happy to do so, and as we drove along, I glanced more closely at him. Suddenly I realised that this was the famous Barry Corey, our school President! The students affectionately referred to him as DBC (D for Doctor). We began a conversation as he inquired who I was, where I came from and what I was studying. That began a long friendship that had him invite my family to his house for dinner.

Lausanne World Congress in Cape Town

Later that year (2010) the Lausanne World Congress was having its congress in South Africa. I wanted to go so badly, but it seemed impossible. Not being in Africa, I had no role in world missions to enable me to join these world leaders to discuss where the church was, with regard to fulfilling the Great Commission. On the other hand, being in the USA, I couldn't afford to pay my way as a USA delegate. My work credentials (cadet!) in the USA was hardly a relevant qualification. I couldn't win either way. The world can really spin in opposite directions at times!

However, as I prayed about it, I was really convinced that I should be in that congress. Gathered there would be many of my colleagues who worked in world mission. It would be a ground-breaking event for evangelists the world over.

As it turned out, DBC i.e. our President was also keen on attending this world gathering. Through his encouragement, Ivan Chung, who was in charge of Global Students, formed a group of students that would attend the forum. He included me in, and that took care of my ticket! However, there were related registration and accommodation costs that needed over $700.

I prayed frantically and asked around. I found out that I could register to go as a steward. If I was willing to 'serve', I could get the benefit of sneaking into the congress with all my accommodation and registration taken care of! God had found a way for me, and I thanked him with all my heart. And so, from October 16 – 25, over 4000 mission leaders from over 198 nations gathered in Cape Town, South Africa. As a steward I arrived early for my steward training.

This was a great occasion. Africa was hosting the world. It was an historical and also quite a nostalgic event, given that in the 1910 Edinburgh World Missionary Conference in UK (referred to as the first documented orld-wide gathering of the Church on missions) there had been NO delegate at all from Africa, only missionaries who worked out there.

Africa plays host

Now, 100 years later, Africa was playing host to its brothers and sisters from around the world! Once the dark continent (in civilization and Christianity), we were now playing a pivotal role in charting the way forward for the future of world Christian missions. What a moment and what a privilege it was to be present to witness this!

When as stewards we were assigned 'stations', I was happy to see myself assigned to be behind the main stage. I was to be among the protocol team assigned to the speakers. That meant I was always at the front (though behind the scenes) and therefore able to listen in to every presentation. God knows our needs!

The Lausanne Congress in Cape Town provided another highlight for me: I had the opportunity of introducing Dr Barry Corey to Michael Cassidy and the leadership of African Enterprise from all over the continent. DBC had a chance to address them, and to share about Biola. I will never forget that day: the two parts of my life had come together: AE and Biola – in Cape Town, of all places! I stood there in my orange steward shirt, just revelling in the joy that I felt to be back among my former colleagues. Meeting them again, given all my upheavals and problems in the USA, was a bit like Joseph seeing his brothers for the first time – without revealing himself. They had no clue of my adventures in the USA, and just assumed everything had gone fine!

After the congress, we flew to Kenya with Dr Corey and Paula his wife. I had arranged for him to meet some former Biola alumni from Kenya. Paula was, in addition, keen to visit some of Kenya's more needy communities, and in particular meet our ByGrace kids of whom she had heard so much.

Back to Biola and back to grim reality: I still had to reckon with my studies and ongoing economic situation. Being away from my work as a cadet had left an even deeper deficiency in my already woeful finances. It also meant catching up on my PhD work. Both ardurous tasks! However, the Lord had a surprise in the offing.

Following my encounter with the Head of Finance, Dr Starcher and Marla Campbell had heard of my tight financial situation and the very possible consequences of discontinuation. They had met and pondered how to rescue me. By now I had 100% tuition scholarship, and they could not engage on what was considered 'personal' student bills – rent, food and the mandatory insurances.

In the course of their deliberations, they suddenly had a happy thought: I had had enormous experience of missions, doing them the length and breadth of Kenya for 16 years. Why not utilise my specialist knowledge by bringing me onto the faculty of the department?

Adjunct faculty

So, I was summoned and asked to apply to become adjunct faculty, and to teach missions.

I was astonished – what a bolt from the blue! Teaching had never occurred to me – that was Rosemary's domain. However, I shared this possibility with Rosemary, and we thanked God for the possibility of such a job. But – first I had to pass the demanding faculty interview. The Talbot school of Theology rightly vetted every lecturer, to ensure their theology was right.

I had been warned this was a tough interview, and it was. But the results did not take long, and I was confirmed as an adjunct faculty.

Due to my academic PhD load, it was agreed that I was to teach over the summer breaks. So, I 'hung in there.' Come 2011 summer, and I taught my first World Missions Course to MDiv students and Masters students. Dr Tom Sappington, who was also one of my PhD instructors, was there to guide me through that first course, as I settled into the new job.

I had to smile to myself at times: becoming a teacher at Biola had been for me such a

bizarre turn of events. I was still working for Campus Safety as cadet all night, but now during the day I was an adjunct faculty. I was on the North and South pole at the same time! Some evenings I would be teaching post-graduates about world mission, and early the next morning, as a Campus Safety cadet, I would be making sure their cars were parked correctly! I could see some keen students had spotted me and were trying to figure out what on earth was going on. In several cases, I explained it to them.

But the funniest and most heart-warming remarks would come from my son Victor – then a teenager: "My dad is both a watchman and a lecturer – oh my ****!" – adding a popular, if crude expletive. But I had to grin at his happy amusement. God was indeed on the move, in ways beyond our understanding!

The best news was that for the two weeks block course, I was paid $3,700. And so, the summer of our 3rd year became a time when the silver lining was clearly evident! At last we had provisions for our various basic needs. But by now we were all too aware that we had come through a wilderness, and the same hand had provided for us there – just as the Israelites in the wilderness. But in our case, we were determined to never forget His past provision.

In the meantime, we knew we had to be wise with our money, to make it last. I could only teach over the summer break. So Rosemary, who has always been our family financial manager, took over the planning as to how we would stay afloat. This still called for faith, granted the many months still to come. So, we were 'there', but 'not yet there'. We had to keep faith and focus on Him!

South Sudan research

2011 was the year to travel, when I was due to travel to South Sudan to collect data for my research. The provision through my Biola teaching therefore saved the day. As a family we first went to Kenya, on a ByGrace summer team. From there, I proceeded to Juba, South Sudan, to interview members of the new South Sudan legislative assembly for my PhD research.

The light at the end of the tunnel, as far as my PhD, was now becoming clear. At last I could spend time engaging with the subjects of my focus area. It was so fulfilling, and the reception accorded to me was also very encouraging. The Vice President, who had once so intimidated me, was now very welcoming. In fact, because he was too busy to meet me during the week, he then invited me over the weekend to his private residence for the interview! This was favour itself, given his busy schedule.

My research questions to him and the other legislators focused around values, norms and motivations of leadership. I ended up interviewing 29 of these legislators and accruing enough data for my research.

When I stepped into the plane on the flight back from Nairobi to Europe, (before heading on to the USA) I heard someone shout out "Steve."

I looked around, and there was the other Steve, my old friend Steven Lungu. As the flight was not full, we ended up sitting together, and doing some good catchup.

Steve was serving then as CEO and International Team Leader for African Enterprise. But he informed me of his intentions to retire the following year. He then challenged me to consider if the Lord could possibly be calling me back to African Enterprise!

My response was that, having served for 16 years at AE was probably good enough, and that God was probably calling me to go somewhere else, though as yet I had no idea where. Stephen Lungu had, however, managed to plant a thought in my mind. Could the Lord possibly want me to go back to AE? It was indeed among the last options I would have thought of.

Back at Biola I settled down to the rigours of compiling my data. By now it was 2012; I had one more year to finish my PhD, within the five years we had set ourselves. Students could go up to seven years, but Rosemary and I had committed to finish within the five year duration. Having begun her studies (through tutorials) a year earlier than I, she had in fact graduated in December 2011, and began her OPT (Optional Practical Training) through ByGrace Trust.

Bolt from the blue

I was equally determined to finish on time. Meanwhile, I had lots of recorded data to transcribe. I was pretty busy, and as Campus Safety was our lifeline, I needed to somehow keep going with that as well. Victor had by now started high school at Sunny Hills in Fulleton, and this meant more lengthy distances to drive each day. Thankfully, Joy was now in Hutchinson Middle-school, literally a stone throw from our Biola apartment.

And then - in 2012, out of the African blue sky, came a phone call from Michael Cassidy. Steven Lungu seemed to have sold me out! Michael and Jonathan Addison (then AE's International Board Chairman) wanted to talk to me. They had gotten wind of the end to my studies being within sight. They were keen to know of my intentions post-Biola.

When I told them that we intended to come back to Africa, they proceeded to inform me that the search for Steven Lungu's successor as AE's International CEO was on and that they were keen to consider me among the various people they were considering, and intending to interview for the position.

I was astounded. Here was yet another bolt from the blue! I shared the news with Rosemary, who equally marvelled. t seemed incredible to us. We had both been so sure that when we left Kenya, that was the end of our time with AE. We had never doubted that during all our time in the USA. And certainly, throughout those five years, AE in Monrovia had never come near us.

But now, AE wanted us back! We had some important choices to make. It was time to pray and gain clarity from the Lord. We needed guidance before making any commitments. We felt like we had come through a long dark tunnel that was suddenly opening into sunshine, and the brightness of the future was almost blinding. But which way should we now go?

With my adjunct faculty title, we reasoned that there were probably possibilities of simply staying on at Biola. I could build a career as a lecturer in Mission, where my background in world missions would be well utilized. By doing so, I would be helping to inform the minds of hundreds and even thousands of students who would in turn be going out to do missions around the world.

Such a job would possibly include a comfortable salary (as seen from my summer classes), regular working hours, a scenic campus with well-equipped classrooms and library – and I could mobilize summer mission groups to Africa like we were already doing. It could be argued that this was a good and godly plan. Plus, our children were now used to the American culture and education system, and could finish their education here, in good schools and colleges.

Called back to Africa

But, while we were not at all sure where we would go in Africa, and what we would do in Africa, and with whom, still, deep in our hearts, we knew that we had made a commitment that we were to go back to Africa. We were happy for our friends who had been called to stay in the USA, as there were many needs here. But for us, we were sure that our true mission base of operation had to be Africa. For one thing, our bigger family of the ByGrace children were waiting for us, and we had to keep our promise to return to our dear friends at the Mathare North church. So, our mind was made up : it had to be Africa.

However, before making up my mind about AE, I decided to take some time to really think it all through. Graduation was still a way off. Also, I needed to understand before God what had happened between me and AE for those long five years. Humanly, I had been hurt by their seeming indifference to me the moment I had left the staff. AE had seemingly deserted me for those critical years. It wasn't the lack of any financial support – I had always understood that. It was the lack of anything in terms of social camaraderie and acknowledgement that I had served them for 16 years. Why had they done that to me?

After much thought and prayer, it gradually seemed clear that it had been God who had taken AE away from me for a time, and for a good reason. I had been with AE for so long that I had come to rely on the organization too heavily for my ministry and my identity. But God had wanted to free me from that, and to help me to learn to rely on Him alone – just as when He called me at the very start of my journey. To move from the possible to the impossible in mobilizing the church for missions required total reliance on Him and Him alone. Hence, these wilderness years in California.

We knew that God was indeed calling us back to Africa. I had been called to go to the unreached myself, not to teach others to go. I also knew that my heart was set on reaching the leadership of Africa. My PhD, with its focus on values and motivations of political leaders, had only served to further inform and cement that passion.

That passion to reach the leadership of Africa was something that I shared with African Enterprise. Its history, from its very beginning in South Africa, as steered by Michael Cassidy, had that same DNA. There was also the mass mobilization for missions by African Enterprise. Through the team in Kenya, I had played a role in enlarging the scope of this in Kenya's cities. The thought I might possibly play a role in encouraging other teams within African Enterprise towards massive mobilization seemed to stir within me.

CEO of African Enterprise

In the end, I didn't have long to think. The chair and International Board of African Enterprise invited me to London for an interview in the month of May 2012. I was to meet with the International Board and present my vision and plan as to where I thought African Enterprise should be headed.

So, I prayed and felt the peace to go. I would present my ambitious plan and leave the results to God. If what I shared was not compatible with their vision of African Enterprise, it would be a good way of at least saying goodbye. I owed AE so much – it had taught me and grown me, from my early days of answering the call to mission.

African Enterprise graciously offered to cover all my expenses for the trip. Meeting the Board was a nostalgic experience, as I had known a good number of them well: Michael Cassidy, Jonathan Addison, Mike Woodall and Steven Lungu, for nearly all my time with African Enterprise.

A few weeks following the interview, I got the formal communication from the chairman Jonathan Addison. It was the Board's decision to appoint me as the 3rd International CEO of African Enterprise.

In August of 2012 African Enterprise was celebrating its 40th anniversary. It was a good time to go back to them. Rosemary, Victor, Joy and I had come over for a short-term mission trip to Kenya, and African Enterprise organized for us all to come down to Pietermaritzburg in South Africa, where the celebrations were happening.

During this celebration, dubbed Jabulani (Rejoice), I was publicly commissioned to be Chief Executive Officer / International Team Leader for African Enterprise.

Passing on the baton of AE

It was a moving moment for me, as Michael (the founder in 1962), Stephen Lungu (the 2nd CEO, 2007-2012) and myself as the 3rd leader of AE stood at the front together in a 'passing of the baton' moment! Here I was, as a 3rd generation evangelist, taking over from these two giants of faith!

2012 was a year of completion for me. Back in California, I was still a cadet, but by now I had risen to Zebra 4 (and honoured as the most outstanding cadet of 2012). I was still an adjunct. Now I was being given a third role: ushered into this weighty role of stewarding African Enterprise's mission of evangelising the cities of Africa with the Good News!

We flew back to USA feeling over the moon and just astounded at how God had worked. I had not only been commissioned, but had assumed the role of AE's CEO, and with some partial stipend while still in the USA , could now concentrate on concluding my studies.

It was time to at last give back my blue Campus Safety cadet uniform, and take on a new uniform! From now on I would 'wear' the 'evangelists all season Good News uniform', that should fit every context from top political leaders to those who felt they were 'the least of these'. The Good News was for all of them!

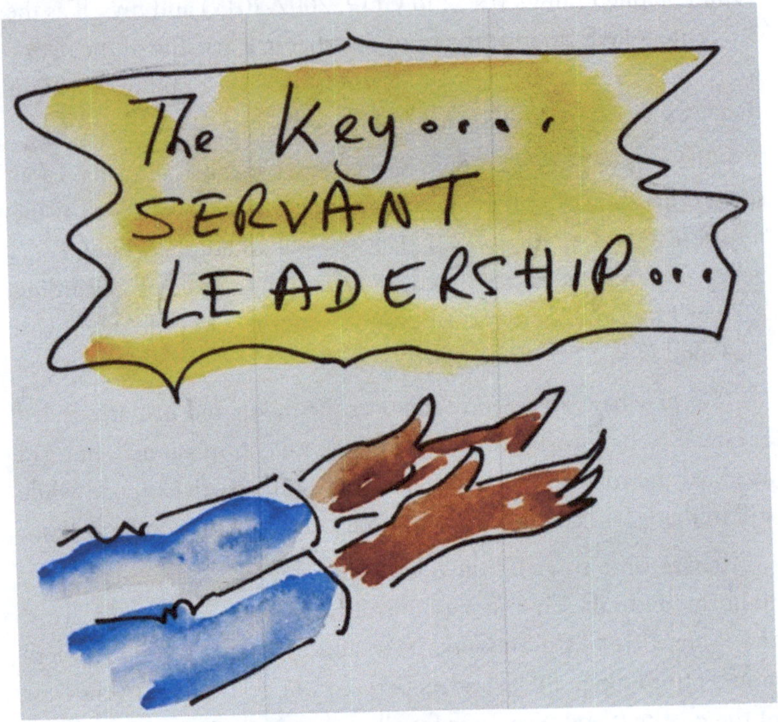
The Key....
SERVANT
LEADERSHIP...

Epilogue

The past eight years has been a time of growing tensions in Africa. Our population is on the rise, our cities are sprawling ever further and further out, and conflict is spreading. China is moving into Africa, eager to help and also get a share of the continent's riches. Islam is on the march across Africa, eager for its soul. The churches in Africa have been deeply impacted by all this, and most of all, by the frightening increase in the persecution of Christians.

More than ever, the leadership and the cities of Africa need to hear the message of the Gospel. If the churches of Africa do not bear witness to Him, who will? That is why African Enterprise has such a passion to help the churches reach the cities of Africa with the Gospel. Our window of opportunity is now, and even so, it is narrowing. (For more on African Enterprises' work check www.africanenterprise.com. And for Rosemary Mbogo's children work: www.bygracetrust.org.)

This book ends here, in August of 2012. Since then I have served as African Enterprise's CEO and International Team Leader (ITL) during some very turbulent times for Africa.

The rest of my story, filling in on these last eight years (2012 to the present day) is due for publication at the end of this year.

If you have enjoyed my story so far and would like to know when the full book is published, please send an email to office@africanharvestpublications. They will then contact you when the book is available.